The Herefordshire Chantry Valuations of 1547

The Herefordshire Chantry Valuations of 1547

The Working Book of William Crowche, Surveyor of Augmentations

Edited by
M. A. Faraday, *MA, FSA*

2012

ISBN: 978-1-291-15640-9

....

By the same Editor

The Westmorland Protestation Returns 1641/2

The Herefordshire Militia Assessments of 1663

The Radnorshire Hearth Tax Return of 1670

Ludlow 1085—1660: A Social, Economic and Political History

The Lay Subsidy for Shropshire 1524-7

The Radnorshire Lay Subsidy Assessment for 1544

Worcestershire Taxes in the 1520s;
The Military Survey and Forced Loans of 1522-3 & the Lay Subsidy of 1524-7

Herefordshire Taxes in the Reign of Henry VIII

The Bristol and Gloucestershire Lay Subsidy of 1523-1527

Calendar of Probate and Administration Acts 1407 – 1550
In the Consistory Court of the Bishops of Hereford

THE HEREFORDSHIRE CHANTRY VALUATIONS OF 1547

INTRODUCTION

In the later Middle Ages it was common for persons with property to endow chantries, chiefly for prayers to be said for the donor or members of his family for the indefinite future. A chantry usually involved paying a stipend to at least one priest for this purpose, sometimes with an altar or shrine or a place set aside for these purposes within a cathedral or a parish church. Typically the endowment would have been land the income from which paid these expenses. Less elaborate endowments for similar purposes were in the form of 'Obits' the income from which was payable to the existing priests of the church as a form of fee for saying prayers, usually in perpetuity. 'Anniversaries' were a form of Obits. Even less elaborate were 'lights'—where small endowments paid for the perpetual or periodical burning of candles. From these endowments churches accumulated properties around the county, sometime in other counties. The endowed properties were often, at the time of their endowment, subject to charges of various kinds, usually chief rents, which had to be paid before the chantry received the dedicated income. The duty of saying prayers often did not keep the chantry priests busy, so very many involved themselves in other activities such as notaries and schoolmasters; local chantry-schools were in fact important local institutions.

Chantries, obits and lights all rested on belief in the doctrine of purgatory from the trials of which intercessionary prayers could obtain relief. Inevitably the Henrician Reformation cut this doctrinal foundation away. Even during the lifetime of Henry VIII measures were being prepared for the abolition of chantries and the expropriation of their properties by the Crown.

In 1547, by virtue of the Act of 1 Edward VI chapter 14, all chantries and their properties were declared to be Crown possessions. Commissioners were appointed to make returns into the Court of Augmentations of the lands and revenues of the chantries, county by county. The records thus created vary, but for Herefordshire there are three, catalogued in The National Archives as E. 301/24, 25 and 26. The first of these is a formal document, set out parish by parish, which usefully gives the number of 'houseling souls' in each parish – that is, the number of communicants—and also various charges upon the income, such as schools and stipends. The second is a similar document covering Herefordshire and Worcestershire. The third of these documents is a 'working' document, full of amendments and corrections, which lists individual properties, either by name or by their occupiers' names, and their immediate new owners, if sales had been made during the working life of the book itself. This edition consists of a transcription of that document with footnotes and an index.

The document is catalogued with the dates '1546-1552'. Clearly the valuations themselves were completed well before 1552. The latter date covers the later annotations describing sales of the properties. But is 1546 correct? Two occupiers are listed who died in late 1546 or early 1547: John Wattes and Richard Taylor of Ledbury (sections 24 and 26 in this edition, and probates 546/261 and 273 in the *Calendar of Probate and Administration Acts 1407-1550 in the Consistory Court of the Bishops of Hereford*—compiled by the present editor). But four occupiers listed in these valuations were clearly the heirs of persons shown in the same probate calendar as having died in late 1546 or early 1547: John Glover of Weobley, son of Agnes (valuation s. 108 and probate 546/12), Margaret Connop of Pembridge, widow of Thomas (s. 195 and 546/66), Richard Harris of Walford, son of John (s. 68, 546/335), Elizabeth Aggas or Hagger of Ross, widow of William (s. 54a-b, 546/338). But conclusive is Thomas Nycolas of Hope-under-Dinmore, whose probate is listed before July 1547 (546/77) and whose gift by will (expropriated by the Crown within weeks of his death!) is listed in s. 94c here. Accordingly the present editor dates these valuations to 1547, made under the Chantry Act of that year, rather than under that of 1545 (37 Hen. VIII, c.4). Wattes and Taylor, though deceased, may have been listed in ignorance of their deaths. The certificate was delivered to the auditor by the deputy surveyor on 19 February 1549 (section 122), but now includes a letter written from the court of Augmentations by its chancellor, Sir Richard Sackvile, on 12 June 1552 (section 109a).

Evidently the lists were made and then annotated as individual properties were sold off. Eventually most or all of the properties were disposed of, but the annotations ceased well before that process was complete. Many of the disposals can be found in the *Calendar of Patent Rolls 1547-53*, but the information there given, although sometimes quite detailed, is grouped under the names of the purchasers and therefore typically includes properties situated in several counties. The index to the published Calendar is not a good example of its kind, so searches for particular properties can take some time. Nevertheless the Calendar can repay the hard work of examining it.

The survey of the Herefordshire chantries was put under William Crowche, Surveyor of Augmentations, whose working book this is. William Sayer was appointed deputy surveyor. Responsibility within the county was sub-divided between three collectors: John Jauncey, collector for Hereford cathedral and City, Radlow, Broxash and Grimsworth hundreds, John Scudamore, collector for Greytree, Wormilow and Webtree (including part of Stretford) and John Incke, collector of Wigmore, Wolphey, Huntington hundreds. Each made a return which was incorporated in the county surveyor's book. There is nothing for the hundred of Ewyas Lacy which may therefore have had no chantries or obits.

The form of the surveys recorded in the book is usually for the caption to be set out in bold lettering at the start of each parish (or chantry) return, but on the left-hand side. In this edition, for clarity's sake, an editorial caption is placed centrally in bold face with the actual caption placed below, not in the margin, but left-justified. The caption is followed by a list of individual properties with their valuations shown on the right with totals for each parish shown, either at the foot of the column, or in the right-hand margin. There then follows a list of 'reprises', preceded by a caption; that is, existing charges on the individual properties above. This list is also totalled in the same way or ways. After that the total of reprises is deducted from the total of valuations above and the net total given.

There are a great many marginal annotations, usually written some time afterwards and mostly indicating to whom the individual properties had been sold. Some groups of properties were sold as single lots and are covered by single annotations. For the most part these annotations were in the right-hand margin, but, where there was insufficient room, annotations also appear in the left-hand margin. In this edition all such annotations have been set centrally below the valuation or reprise to which they relate and set in a slightly smaller type-face.

The substance of the return is almost wholly in English, but most annotations are in Latin. Roman numerals are used throughout for valuations and totals. Where it seems necessary—and is possible—translations or summaries of the Latin are given in footnotes. These annotations are often abbreviated and scribbled, so some are indecipherable or can only be guessed.

Most lines in the valuations are annotated with 'ex' and/or 'pr', standing for 'examinatur' and/or 'probatur' (examined and checked). Because of their number in this edition they are set down only as 'e' and 'p'. Many of the parish returns are followed by faint auditors' use grids, a form of 'abacus' using dots set into a rough grid, the whole representing figures, according to the rules of the 'use'. Those which are clear have been included here; those which are not have been left out. The entire text is abbreviated according to the conventions of the time; in this edition all abbreviations have been extended, but the editorial extensions are set in italic. Other editorial additions are shown within square brackets [ ].

The original return uses a sequential numbering system for the returns. This however is deficient; some returns have no numbers, while others are repeated. In this edition the original numbers are adopted, but unnumbered chantry returns have been given other numbers, usually alphabetical suffixes. This is particularly the case with Cathedral chantries and obits. The index uses these numbers as editorially adjusted.

The absence of text through tearing is shown thus [***]; if the missing text can be supplied through the exercise of common sense or by analogy it will be shown thus [*John]. Where text is present but cannot be deciphered it is shown thus [...]. Editorial interpretations which may be doubtful are preceded by '?'.

The text includes a great deal of crossings out. Where the words or figures so crossed out can still be read they are shown here with a line struck through.

Many entries in parish returns are preceded or followed by marks, such as •, or +; this practice is clearly to indicate properties which were treated together, usually sold together as a single lot.

This record is of interest to scholars of the 16th century, particularly of the post-Reformation secularisation of Church property. In addition, family historians, once they have reached the mid-16th century from which period parish registers and collections of wills are very much more sparse, must of necessity look at any lists of residents in particular places and this is one. Being a 'working document' it is somewhat unusual, being both a record of properties and a record of their disposals. This edition therefore includes a detailed index of the properties, their occupiers and of the early purchasers and grantees.

Much of the work on this transcription was done many years ago when the document was still at the old Public Record Office in Chancery Lane. It is now at The National Archives at Kew who retain copyright in the document on behalf of the Crown.

I should like to record my gratitude to two friends; first, to Dr James G Nourse who generously gave me unrestricted access to the materials which he had collected, thus enabling me to check and augment the transcriptions which I had made some thirty years before; secondly to Alan O'Brien, who has given me the benefit of his experience in preparing texts for publication and, indeed, who has actually handled the process. I could not have finished the work, still less published it, without their essential help, and I remain very grateful to them both.

M. A. FARADAY
Walton-on-Thames

ABBREVIATIONS

CPR	*Calendar of Patent Rolls*
CSPD	*Calendar of State Papers Domestic*
E. 301	Exchequer—Augmentations: Certificates of Colleges and Chantries
Hereford Probates	M. A. Faraday (ed.): *Calendar of Probate and Administration Acts 1407-1550 in the Consistory Court of the Bishops of Hereford* (2009)
Herefordshire Taxes	M. A. Faraday (ed.): *Herefordshire Taxes in the Reign of Henry VIII (Woolhope N.F.Club, 2005)*
TNA	The National Archives

GLOSSARY

ad usum	for the purposes of
allocatur	it is allowed
ballivatus	bailiwick or division of a county
ballivus	bailiff
cancellatur	it is cancelled
cantaria	chantry
conceditur	it is granted
firma decimarum	farm of the tithes
dictus	the said
dominus Rex, *dat.* domino Regi	the Lord King
elemosina	alms
examinatur	it is examined; (shown as) 'e:'
exoneratur	it is discharged
extinguitur	it is extinguished
fenum	hay
feodum firmum	fee farm
festum Pascalis	Easter
generosus, *dat.* generoso	gentleman
granum	grain
imperpetuum, in perpetuum	for ever
in litteris patentibus	in Letters Patent
miles, *dat.* militi	knight
notatur	it is noted
oneratur	it is charged
orreum	barn
parochia	parish
per eosdem	by the same
perquisitum	purchase
perquisitor	purchaser
per rationem unionis possessionum	by reason of the merger of ownership
prefatus	aforesaid
probatur	it is proved (checked); (shown as) 'p:'
quo jure	by what right
redditus	rent
sic remanet clare	so there remains clear
solvitur	it is paid
summa	sum or total
summa de claro	clear total (net sum)
ut supra	as above
venditur	it is sold
venduntur	they are sold
vicecomes, *gen.* vicecomitis	sheriff

CHANTRY VALUATION CERTIFICATE OF 1547
The Working Book of William Crowche, Surveyor of Augmentations

[*The National Archives, E. 301/26*]

Herefordshire

f.[i] **00** The Chantres in the Cathedrale Church of Hereford, the Ch*a*untryes in the Citie of Heref*ord,* The Ch*a*untres in the Hundred*e*s of Radlowe, Broxshashe & Grymyswood: Collected by John Jaunceye [1]

[f.1] The Countie of Hereford
The certyfycath of Will*iam* Crowche surveyor unto the kyng*e*s maieste within the county of Herefford of all the land*e*s meadowes leasowes & pastures wood*e*s & underwood*e*s rentes rev*er*cyons & servic*e*s belongyng to the chaunt*er*eys & stypend*i*ary servic*e*s beyng lately dissolvyd & lately app*er*teynyng to the cathedrall churche of Heref*ord* w*ith*in the countye of Hereff*ord* as hereafter ensuythe [2]

No.**1** The Counties of Wiltes*hire* & Oxford
In p*r*imis the Chaunt*er*ey of O*u*r Ladye w*ith*in O*u*r Lady Chapell called Byshopp*e* Audeles Chaunt*er*ey admountyng to the valure of viii £. partycules wheroff be not c*er*tyfyed her ffor that that the same land*e*s lying ffor in countys [3]

Rec*eptus* ?in*tra* Revent*iones* Com*itatus* Wilte*n*sis & Oxo*niensis* [4]

Hereford Cathedral: S. George's Chantry

No.**2** The Rentall of the land*e*s belongyng to the Chaunt*ery* of S.Georg*e* w*ith*in the Cathedrall Churche above sayd
In p*r*imis John Bromwhiche gent holdyth certen landes meadowes leasowes & pastures lying in the paryshe of Founhope caled the Garlande — iiii £.
vend*itur* Rog*ero* Herefford [5] & Johan*ni* P*r*idieux [6] e: p:
It*em* Elyzabethe Vycares wedowe holdythe a brewe howse in Brodcabage Lane in the Cytye of Heref*ord* and pay*e*the yerelye — xiiis.iiiid.
[*Total*] iiii £. xiiis. iiiid.
where[*of]

[f.1v] Rep*r*ises
In p*r*imis the p*r*este of the sayd chaunt*er*ey paythe yerely to the kyng*e*s ma*ies*tie for a quytt rent owte of the sayd brewhowse — xiid.
no*tatur* quo jure xiid.solvit*ur* D*omi*no Regi sol*uta* ball*ivo* ~~ville~~ Civ*itatis* Hereff*ordie* ut p*er* an*nua*le feod*um* firm*um* ut ?d*ictus* p*er* deput*atem* sup*ervisoris* [7]
It*em* the sayd p*r*est pay*e*the yerely owt of the same brewhowse to the deane & chapytor of Herefford — xiid.
It*em* the same prest pay*e*the yerely oute of all the seyd land*e*s to the mayntaynyng of i obytte yerely in the sayd cathedrall churche for hys foundres soules — ~~xiiis. iiiid~~.
cancellat*ur* q*uia* nec*n*on alloc*atur*
[*Total reprises*] ~~xvs. iiiid~~. iis. p :
Et remanet clar*e* [8] ~~vii £~~. ~~Lxxviiis~~. e: iiii £. xis. iiiid. e:

---

[1] Deputy surveyor responsible for these hundreds within the county.
[2] Since John Jauncey was responsible for the valuations of cathedral chantry property and William Crouch does not appear to have certified any other properties, this is an odd item. All the other valuations were examined by William Sayer, Crouch's deputy. Jauncey was however also recorded as a deputy surveyor, (see section 53e).
[3] This has the appearance of something read over but misheard; clearly "lie in foreign counties" was meant and doubtless said.
[4] These properties were dealt with in the Wiltshire and Oxfordshire surveys.
[5] Of Sutton, (*CPR, iii, 258*).
[6] Of the Inner Temple, (*Ibid.*).
[7] By what right is the quit rent paid to the lord king paid by the bailiff of the City of Hereford as a yearly fee-farm.
[8] The meaning is in English 'clear' but in this document there is neither consistency nor correctness, 'de claro' is the best version, but 'declaro' is also used, along with 'clara' clare', and claro', after 'summa' or 'remanet' and without the preposition. As the word is usually abbreviated to 'clar', in this edition this has been extended to 'clare', even though incorrect, on the footing that this was usually intended.

In p*ri*mis ther belongyng to the seyd chaunt*ery* c*er*ten land*es* meadowes lesues & pastures admountyng to the yerely valure of iiii £. whych are not retorned her for that that the sayd landes lying forin countye [9] in the countie of Essex

Re*ceptus* int*ra* Revent*iones* Com*itatus* Essexe[10]

Hereford Cathedral: Our Lady Chantry

No. **3** The Rentall of all the land*es* & ten*ement*es belongyng to the Chaunt*ery* of O*ur* Lady w*ith*in the cath*edral* churche of Herefford

In p*ri*mis Wil*lia*m Mason holdyth on*e* ten*emen*te *with* the appe*r*ten*an*c*es* lying in Moch Cowarn by the rent [11] L.s.

vend*itur* Jo:[*hanni*] Pe*r*ient & Thome Reve [12] e: exone*ratur*

It*em* John Skydmor esquyer holdyth land & medowes & pastur*es* lying in Hom Lacye xxxvs. iid. p:

conc*editur* Jo:[*hanni*] Cupp*er* & Ric*ardo* Travor [13]

It*em* John Kery holdyth landes lying in Portfyld a lytle medo lying by the seyd Portfyld one other lytle medo lying bye Nyghtynghalhall & ii acres of errable land lying in the Lytle Portfyld w*ith* a c*er*ten closse called Avescroft ~~& paythe~~ Lxvs. e:

vend*itur* Rogers & Veale de Heref*ordie*

It*em* S*ir* John Yaydon & John Dornell pay*e*th for ye chant*ery* howse xiiis. iiiid.

vend*itur* W:[*illelmo*] Britton & Ambrose Nicholas

It*em* John Nurse holdyth land*es* & medowes & pastur*es* lying at Weston under Penyord xxiiis.iiiid.

vend*itur* Jacobo Rogers & R[*icardo*] Veale

ix £. vis. xd.

[f.2] Rep*ri*ses

In p*ri*mis Will*ia*m Mason pay*e*th oute of hys ten*emen*te to Morice Bartley for a cheffe rente iiis. iiiid.

exone*ratur* per Jo:[*hannem*] Perient & Tho:[*mam*] Reve

Item payd to M*aste*r John Scudamore for the seyd land*es* as to hys man*or* off Hom Lacye xxiid.

p*er* Jo:[*hannem*] Cupp*er* [&] Ric*ard*um Trevor exon*eratur* p*redictos*

Item ~~the seyd~~ John Kerye pay*e*the yerely to the kynges maiestie for cheffe rent forthe sayd Portfyld & the sayd ii lytle meadowes lying besyde Portfyld afore sayd iis. vid.

sol*vitur* extingu*itu*r no*tatu*r Rogers & Veale vend*itores* exon*erant* iis. vid.
payde to the kynges ma*ie*stie tu*m* modo extinct*um* p*er*
rat*ione*m union*is* possess*ionum* Ideo ... [14]
No*tatu*r quo jure sol*vitur* d*omi*no Regi redd*itus* iis. vid.
sol*vitur* ball*ivo* ~~ville~~ Civi*tat*is Hereff*ordie* ut sup*ra*

Item the same John Kerye paythe yerely for the sayd ii acres off errable lands and the closse called Aves crofte errable ground lykewysse to the deane & chapyter of Herefford iis. vid. e:

exon*eratur* p*er* Rogers & Veale

Item the p*ri*est of the sayd chaunt*er*ye payethe yerely oute of the same chaunt*ery* howse to the M*aste*r of the Almeshowse iiiid.

exon*eratur* p*er* W:[*illelmum*] Britten & Ambrosium Nicholas [15]

Item John Nurse pay*e*the yerely owte of the land*es* meadowes & pastures lying in Weston aforsayd to the Baylye of Greytre to the use of the kynges maieste xvid. e:

exon*eratur* p*er* Rogers & Veale
N*otatu*r ubi profit*a* terr*arum* in Greytre s*olvita*
d*omi*no Regi ad man*um* vice*comitis* com*itatus* Hereff*ordiensis* [16]

---

[9] Evidence of a copyist mishearing what was being read over to him. Clearly what was said was "lie in a foreign county".

[10] Received in the revenues of Essex.

[11] Tenement belonged to William Mason, Roger his son & Joan , Roger's wife. (*CPR, iii, 10).*

[12] Thomas Reve of London, (*CPR, iii, 376*).

[13] Of London, (*CPR*, iii, 396).

[14] Because the rent was payable to the king from property now taken by the king (by union of possession) it is extinguished.

[15] Both of London, (*CPR, iii, 142*).

[16] Note where profits of land in Greytree due to the lord king are paid into the hands of the sheriff of the county of Hereford.

Item the said chaunt[*r*]ie priest paied out of his house to the
Kynges baylif & Comonalte of the Citie of Hereford yerely vid.

exoner*atur* per W:[*illelmum*] Britten & Ambros*ium* Nicholas

Notatur ~~ut supra~~

[*Total reprises*] xiis. iiiid.

Et remanet clar*e* viii £. xiiiis. vid.

Hereford Cathedral: Kentisburcote Chantry

[f.2v] **4.** The Rentall of all the land*es* & ten*emente*s belongyng to the cha*unter*y of Kentysburcote w*ith*in the cathedrall Church of Herefford

In pr*i*mis a ten*emen*te w*ith* the land*es* called Burcote in the tenure of John Webbe by rent by yere Ciiis. iiiid.

vend*itur* W:[*illelmo*] Cicell & L[*awrence*] Eresbye

Item a ten*emen*te in Shelwycke in the tenure of Thom*as* Andros by yere xs.

Item a lytle closse in Shelwycke in the tenure of John Leche xiid.

vend*itur* Reve et Johnson

Item one other ly*t*tle ^ close [^] ther in the tenure of Rog*er* Hynton xiid.

exoner*atur* e: vend*itur*

Item a ten*emen*te in Castell Strette w*ith* a garden in the tenure of John P*ar*ker vis. viiid.

Castle Streete

Item on*e* other ten*emen*te in the same strette in the tenure off Thomas Smythe iiis.

Item one other ten*emen*te in the same strett in the tenure off John P*ar*ker xxd.

[*Total*] vi £. vis. viiid. p:

whereof: Rep*ri*ses

In p*ri*mis payd out of the ten*emen*te & land*es* of Burcote by yere to the Bysshop of Herefford xls. p:

exoner*atur per* W:[*illelmum*] Cicell & Eresbye

Item payd oute of the thre tenementes lying in the Castell Strete belongyng to the sayd chaunt*ery* to the deane & chapyter by yere iiiis.

[*Total reprises*] xliiiis.

Et reman*et* clar*e* iiii £. iis. viiid. p:

Hereford Cathedral: St. Catherine's Chantry

[f.3] **5.** The Rentall of all the land*es* belongyng to the Chaunt*er*ey of S. Kateryng annexed to the cat*hedral* Church of Her*eford*

In p*ri*mis a yerely pensyon goyng oute of the late monasterye of Wygmor payd nowe by M*aste*r Will*iam* Sheldon the kyng*es* maiestys recevor ~~Liiis. iiiid~~.

canc*ellatur* q*uia* extinguit*ur* r*at*ione uni*onis* possession*um* [17]

Item a yerely pensyon goyng oute of the late monastery of Glocester p*a*yd by the vycare of Foye xls.

Item a yerely rent oute of the prebend of Gorwall payd by Sir John Prese & Wylyam Furny baker xxxs.

And by Wyllyam Furny baker xs.

Item a c*er*ten teythe of Shelwycke payd by M*aste*r John Warmecombe xiiis. iiiid.

Item a ten*emen*te in Brodstrett in the tenure of Wyllyam Dune xiis. e:

vend*itur* Joha*nn*i ~~Ed~~ Butler & Hugoni P*ar*tridge [18]

Item one other ten*emen*te in the same strett in the tenure of John Pynnocke xiis.

Item a ten*emen*te in Sant ~~Andrewes~~ ^ Owyns [^] p*ar*eshe in the tenure of Hughe Adams vis. viiid.

[17] The property of both payer and recipient were now in the hands of the king (union of possession) so payment is extinguished.

[18] Sir John Butler of Great Badminton & Hugh Partridge of London, (*CPR, iii, 280*).

It*em* a annuall rent of M*aste*r Hughe Welshe for the howse
wher he nowe dwellyth xiiis. e:

~~exoneratur~~ vend*itur* Ja*cobo* Rogers & Veale [19]

It*em* a annuall rent of on*e* Walt*er* Morgan for the howse
that he dwellythe in in Wydm*er*she Strete iiis. vid. e:

It*em* a annuall rent of the chaunt*ery* p*ries*t off Saynt Martens
payd by the hand*es* of Rob*er*t Goodma*n* for the howse
wher in he nowe dwellythe ~~iis. iiid.~~

Not*atur* oner*atur* in on*ere* Cantaria B*ea*te Marie
in p*a*rochi*a* S*anc*ti Martini [20]

It*em* annuall rent payd by ye Prec[*e*]ntors of Saint Nycolas for
the house yat Will*ia*m Rawlyng*es* dwellyth in iiiid. ob.

Item ^ ~~iii~~ one [^] small garden ? ~~plock in~~ in the tenure of Hughe
Gybbons xxd.

[f.3v] Item on*e* other in the tenure of M*aste*r Wil*lia*m Barkley iis. iiiid.

Item i other in the tenure of Thomas Churche iiis. vid.

Item too chambers in the tenure of the incu*m*bent*es* rent by yere vis. viiid. p:

g. [21] vend*itur* Jo*hanni* Butler & Hugoni Partridge

[*Total*] ~~xvii £.[+++]~~ vii £. ~~xvs. ob~~. p: [22]

ult*ra* Liiis. iiiid. & iis. iiid. al*iter* ex*aminata*
~~x £. viiis. iiiid. x £. xs. viid. ob~~. [23]

wherof : Rep*ri*ses

In *pr*imis payd to the late P*ri*or of Langtony but now to the
kyng*es* maiestye ~~vs~~.

extinguit*ur* canc*ellata* q*uia* extinguit*ur*
non istud allo*catur* Jo:[*hanni*] Butler mil*iti* &
Hugoni P*ar*tridge gen*er*os*is* in p*er*quis*itis*
ideo p*er* eosdem exon*eratur* etc

Item to the deane & chapyter of Herefford iis. vd.

Item to the kynges Baylyff for a garden viiid.

non q*uia* sol*vitur* d*omi*no Regi ball*ivo* Civ*ita*tis Hereff*ordie*

[*Total Reprises*] ~~v~~iiis. id. p:

Remanet clare ~~x £. iis. vid. ob.~~ ~~xvd. ob~~. e:

Rem*anet* vii £. vis. xid. ob. [24] p:

Hereford Cathedral: Vicars Choral Obits

6. The Land*es* & Re*nt*es of all such Obytt*es* that belongyth to ye Vycars of the
Quyer w*ith*in the cath*edral* Churche of Her*eford*

In p*ri*mis of Thomas Wylcock*es* of Her*eford* for ~~a~~ on*e* medowe
lying by Putteston app*er*teynyng to the obytt of John Falx xs. p:

vend*itur* Rogers & Veale

It*em* of Thomas Bermyngton for a pasture lying by Wydm*er*she
belongyng to the obytte of John Galey vs. e:

vend*itur* eisd*em* Rogers & Veale

Item of Hughe Maredythe for a mese & a garden lying in
Wydm*er*she Strete belongynge to the obytte of Wyllyam
Kedward by yere & above all charges vis. viiid. e:

vend*itur* eisdem Rogers & Veale [25]

Wydmersh Streete

Item of Hughe Walshe for a garden ~~grounde~~ lying in Worthall
belongyng to the obytte of Treamor Flecher ov*er* all charges viiis. e:

vend*itur* eisdem Rogers & Veale

---

[19] This and the next item bracketed to this marginal note.

[20] See section 16.

[21] In the left hand margin a ‘g’ with a superscript flourish after it. Meaning unknown.

[22] The amended total in the right hand margin has the figures after the £7 struck through, which may have been over-enthusiastic, since the actual total seems to be £7 5s. 0½d.

[23] The total of £7 15s. 0½d. and the following line appear in the right hand margin of the previous page, but a bracket extended onto this page makes it clear that the the first three items on page 3v belong within the bracket. The marginal note has therefore been shown here.

[24] The total, after taking account of struck through items, should be £7 11s. 11½d.

[25] This and the next item are linked by bracket to the statement ‘sold to Rogers & Veale’, which is repeated in this edition.

Item of Nycholas Francke for a certen tenement & a garden lying in Hungrye Strette xs. viiid.

[f.4] Item of John Garwey for a yerely rent goyng owte of a ten*emen*te lying in Cokyng ~~Wood~~ ^ Rowe [^] belongyng to the obyte of Roger Norman viiis. xid.

It*em* iiii sev*er*all ten*emen*tes under on*e* ruffe with ii gardens to the same in the Castell Strette belongyng to the obyte of John Wynd & Agnes hys wyffe the rent by yere xixs.

It*em* of Wyllyam Showmaker for a ten*emen*t w*ith* a garde*n* lying in the sayd cytye in a strette called Saynt Owens Strete belongyng to the obytt of Wyllyam Glover viiis.

Item of John Warmecombe esquyer for a garden with a co^l[^]v*er*howse belongyng to ^ the[^] Crosse obytte viis.

It*em* of Will*ia*m Mathowe for a ten*emen*te w*ith* a garden lying in Wybrigstrette belongyng to John Drap*er*s obyt viiis.

vend*itur* Rogers & Veale [26]

It*em* of Hughe Gybbons for a medow lying at Lugge Brydge belongyng Monyworthes obytt viiis.

+It*em* of Johan Chemister for a ten*emen*t in the Narrow Cabage Lane belongyng to Rob*ert* Mastersones obytte viiis.

It*em* of David Jones for a ten*emen*te belongyng to M*aste*r Harvys obyte xiiis. iiiid.

+It*em* of John Barn for a stalle with a garden belongyng to the obytte of John Dore vs.

Item of Rychard Halle al*ia*s Smyth for a garden ^ & one [^] mese lying in Blackm*ar*ston belongyng to the same obyte iiiis.

vend*itur* W:[*illelmo*] Britten & Ambros*io* Nicholas

Item of Wyllyam Denby for a garden belongyng to John Bulkers obytte iis. iiiid.

Item of Will*ia*m Caldycote for a mes*e* w*ith* a garden in Blakm*ar*ston belongyng to John P*ar*sons obytte vis. viiid.

vend*itur* Reve & Johnson

Item of John Ludbye for a ten*emen*te w*ith* a garden lying in the Castell Strette belongyng to Rowlyng Cokes obyte vis. viiid. e:

vend*itur* Rogers & Veale

Item of Ric*hard* Warmecombe for a orchard lying above Ygn belongyng to Rychard Judde & Androw Jones obyte xs.

[f.4v] Item of Mauld Welford wedowe for a ten*emen*te with a garden in Hungry Strette ^ in the citie of Hereford [^] belongyng to Rychard Grenweys obytte <u>xs.</u>

[*Total*] viii £. [*vs.] iiid. p: [27]

wherof: Rep*r*ises

In p*r*imis to M*aste*r Barowe for the cheffe rent of the meadowe lying in Putteston iiid.

exon*eratur per* Rogers & Veale

Item a che*ff*e rent goyng owte of the garden lying in Worthall to the M*aste*r of Thalmeshowse xiid.

exon*eratur per* eosdem Rogers & Veale

Item a quytt rent goyng owte of the seyd ten*emen*te in Cokyngrowe to the kyng*e*s bayll*e*s of the seid citie xiid.

Item p*ai*d to the ~~kyng~~ ^ said bayll*i*s [^] out of the iiii ten*emen*tes in Castell Stret under one ruffe iis. viiid.

Item p*ai*d to S*ir* John a Prece for a chefe rent going out of a garden w*ith* a cover howse [28] xiid.

Item to the same S*ir* John Aprece for a chefe rent going oute of a ten*emen*te w*ith* a garden in the tenure of Wyllyam Showmaker xid. ob.

---

[26] This marginal note also applies to the next item being linked by bracket

[27] The total (and the word 'wherof') appears after a bracket on the previous page linking items on that page with the first item on this page.

[28] Culverhouse or dovecote.

Item for a quytte rent p*ai*d to the M*aste*r of Thalmeshowse for a
howse in the Cabage Lane xiiiid.
Item p*ai*d for a quytte rent to the kyng*es* Bayly for the house in
the tenure of Wyllyam Denbye iiiid.
no*tatur* q*uo* jure sol*vitur* d*omi*no Regi iiiid.
Item p*ai*d for a mes*suage* or ten*emen*te lying in Blakm*ar*ston late
in the tenure of Wyllyam Caldycote iis. iiiid.
exone*ratur per* Reve & Johnson
no*tatur* ? d*om*ini sol*vitur* iis. iiiid. sol*vit* ball*ivo* Civ*ita*tis p*redicte*
[*Total reprises*] xs. viiid. [* ob.] p:.
Reman*et* clar*e* p: vii £. xiiiis. vid. ob.

Hereford Cathedral: Chantries and Vicars Choral Obits: Totals

[6a] S*u*m tot*a*l of the forsaid Ch*aun*tres the Rep*r*ises nott
deducted ~~xxxix £. vd. ob.~~ xxxvi £. viis. id. ob. p:
ultra Liiis. iiiid. pens*io* de mo*nasterio* de
Wigmor extinguit*ur* [***] ?antedi*citur*
The tot*a*l Rep*r*ises Lxx~~v~~iis. id. ob. [29]
And so rem*ains* Clere ~~xxxv £. iiis. iiiid.~~ xxxii £. xvs. p: [30]

Hereford Cathedral: Canons' and Petty Canons Obits

[f.5] The Obyttes & Profettes belongyng to the Cannons & Petye Cannons Vicars in the
Quyer of the sayd Cathedrall Churche of Heref*ord* in the Cytye of Herefford

Hereford Cathedral: Philip Russell's Obit

[6b] Obytt of Felyp Russ*ell*
In p*ri*mis an annuall rent oute of the comen rentes belongyng
to the Deane & Cannons of the seyd cathedrall church yerely
for the obytt*es* of Phylypp Russ*er* xiiis. iiiid. p:

Hereford Cathedral: Roger Cauckbridge's Obit

[6c] The Obytt of Roger Cauckbrydge
The annuall rent oute of the vycarage of the quyer called
Calkbridge vicarage founded at the awter of St. Nycolas
the obytt of Roger Cauckbridge by payd by the vycar of
the same yerely vs.
Also an yerely rent oute of the land*es* of Thomas Morys
of Cobhall in the sayd countye yerely iis. viiid.
In p*ri*mis a yerely rent goyng owte of the land*es* of on*e*
Rychard Symons of Cobball aforseyd yerly xxd.
Item an annuall rent owte of the landes of James ^ Bell [^]
of the same place yerely iiis. iiid. ob.
Item an annuall rent owte of the land*es* of Harrye Wadden yerely iis. iiiid.
Item oute of the land*es* of William Foote yerely iid.
[*Total*] xvs. id. ob. p:

Hereford Cathedral: John Stanbury's Obit

[6d] The Obytt of John Stanbury
In p*ri*mis the annuall rent goyng owte of the vycarage in the
quyer of the seyd cath*edral* churche called Stanburyes
vycarage payd yerely by the vycare fo*r* the tyme beyng yerely xxxs. e:

---

[29] Originally Lxxviis. id. was written, but the 'v' has been struck through.

[30] The second and correct total here has been written across the gutter and is therefore on f.5r. These are the supposed totals for sections 2 to 6 inclusive, as the total for the Reprises confirms, but the errors embodied in the valuation-list for Our Lady chantry make the determination of the actual totals impossible.

Hereford Cathedral: Richard Randall's Obit

[f.5v] **[6e]** The Obytt of Rychard Randdall

The rent of a garden lying in the Cytye of He[*reford] in the parysh of Saynt Peters nowe in the ten[*ure] of John Hunt ~~walker~~ & Rychard Walker payt[*he] [31] [* xviiis.]

[*Reprises*] [32]

Payd yerely for cheff rent unto S*ir* John Prece knyght oute off the sayd garden iis. viiid.

exoner*atur per* Rogers & Veale

And so remaynethe xvs. iiiid.

M*emorandum* that the obyt of Roger Hore & John Pratte ys charged withe [33] chaunter*e*y of O*ur* Ladye in Stoke Edythe in the sayd countye of the yerely value of xxs.in the same ^some [^] of vii £. xiiis. iiiid. no*tatur* [34]

Hereford Cathedral: Peter Radnor's Obit

[6f] The Obytte of Pet*e*r Radnor

The annuall rent oute of a ten*emen*te belongyng to the De*a*ne & Chapyter lying in the cytye of Her*eford* in the tenure of Pet*e*r Vaune & William Luson ii cannons ther yerely [35] xxs. e:

Hereford Cathedral: Ralph Hanning's Obit

[6g] The Obyte of Rauff Han*n*yng

An annuall rent going owte of c*er*ten land*e*s lying in Nuppyn in the p*ar*yshe of Fowne Hop*e* in the countye of Her*eford* in the tenure of Rychard Brydge yerely xiiis. iiiid. e:

Hereford Cathedral: Adam Esegar's Obit

[6h] Berk Shere: The Obytt of Adam Esgar Bysshoppe [36]

The annuall rent going out of the benefys off Shymryngfyld [37] in the countye of Berk *shere* payd by the M*aste*r of the workes of the sayd cath*edral* churche yerely Cs. e:

Hereford Cathedral: Edmund Audley's Obit

[6i] Oxford Shere: Obyt off [*Edmun]d Audeley

The annuall rent goyng owte of c*er*ten land*e*s & ten*emen*tes in the countye of Oxford lying in the p*ar*yshe of Garsyngton ~~xxs~~.

allo*catur quia* oner*atur* coram audit*ore* d*omi*ni R*e*g*is* Oxon*iense* [38]

Hereford Cathedral: David Jack, John Bakon and Sir John Mores's Obit

[6j] The Obytt of Davyd Jacke John Bakon & Sir John Mores founded in the seyd Cathedrall Churche [39]

[***] The annuall rent goyng oute of the canonycall [***]ise lying in the cytye of Hereford in Cabany Lane now [***] the tenure of John Starnyn Archeadeacon of [*Herefo]rd [40] yerely xiiis. iiiid.

---

[31] The corner of this page is torn off and with it the amount of the rent, but this can be supplied as a balancing figure of £12s. 8d. This item was at the foot of the previous page but was linked to the caption by a bracket in the left hand margin.

[32] There is no caption here but editorial clarity requires one to be inserted.

[33] 'with the' obviously intended; haplography.

[34] See section 23b.

[35] Vaune held the prebend of Cublington or Madley, while Luson, the treasurer, held that of Church Withington, (*Fasti, 62-3*).

[36] Adam Esegar of Ledbury was a prebendary of the cathedral until 1369. There is no evidence that he was ever a bishop either in Hereford or elsewhere (*Hereford Cathedral: a history*. ed. G. Aylmer & J. Tiller, 2000, 218). I owe this reference to Brian S Smith.

[37] Not identified, possibly Shillingford.

[38] Allowed (and struck out here) because charged before the king's auditor in Oxfordshire.

[39] This heading appears on the next page but is linked by a bracket with the last entry on this page.The left hand lower corner of the page has been torn off.

[40] John Styrmin, archdeacon of Hereford 1542-1551.

[f.6] The annuall rent going oute of the vicarage called Seynt Agnes vycarage p*ai*d by S*ir* Henry Perpoynt vicare of the quyer in the cathedrall churche of Hereford xs.
The annuall rent goyng out of the canons backhowse of the sayd church payd by [^] the [^] offycer of the seyd backhouse vs. xd.
The annuall rent goyng out of the canon rent belongyng to the Deane & Cannons xiid.
The annuall rent goyng out of the treasure of the sayd cathedrall churche xiid.
[*Total*] xxxis. iid. p:

Hereford Cathedral: John Boyle and John Fystar's Obit

[6k] The Obytt of John Boyle & John Fystar found by them in the seyd Cath*edral* Church of Her*eford* [41]
The medowe lying in Sutton in the countye of Hereford late in the tenure of Rychard Warmecombe decessed yerely xs.
In p*ri*mis the rent of a garden & land*es* belongyng to the sayd obytte lying in the Subbers in the seyd Cytye in the tenure of Will*iam* Burley deceassed & nowe in the tenure of John Bayle pay*e*th yerely xxiis. e:
vend*itur* Rogers & Veale
[*Tota*l] xxxiis. p:
wherof:
Goyng oute of the sayd obytt unto the late monastr*y* of Langtonye [***]
extinguit*ur* *ra*tione union*is* possession*um*
And so reman*eth* [***]

Hereford Cathedral: Philip Haye, Adam Esgar, Robert Geffres and Robert Barnes's Obit

[6l] The Obitt founded by Philip Haye, Adam Esgar, Rob*ert* Geffres and Rob*ert* Barne*s* in the said Cathedrall Churche [42]
It*em* the annuall rent goyng oute of the comon[***] rent*es* of the Dean*e* & Canons of the seyd Chu[***] Hereff[+ord y]erely [*xxxs.] [43]
[f.6v] It*em* the rent ~~parcell~~ of [^] a p*ar*cell of [^] c*er*ten land*es* lying in Nuppyn in the p*ar*yshe of Fowne Hope in the sayd countye in the tenure of Will*iam* Bridge xxs. p:
vend*itur* Jac:[*obo*] Rogers & Veale
It*em* the ^annuall[^] rent goyng oute of a medo lying in Hom Lacy in the sayd countye in the tenure of John Skydmor esqu*y*er xs. e:
vend*itur* Jo:[*hanni*] Cupp*er* & Ric*ardo* Travor exon*eratur*
It*em* a garden & a stable in the back syde of a howse lying in Cabage Lane in the sayd cytyaye[44] & extendyng to the Brodstrete nowe in the tenure of Hughe Barbor yerely vis. viiid. e:
vend*itur* Rogers & Veale
Cabage Lane neere Broad Streete
[*Total*] Lxvis. viiid.

Hereford Cathedral: William Chapman and John Orleton's Obit

[6m] The Obyt founded by Will*iam* Chapman & John Orleton in the seyd Cath*edral* Churche
It*em* the rent of a howse lying in the north gate in the sayd cytye of Heref*ord* late in the tenure of Lewes Spycer & pay*e*the yerely xxiis. e:
vend*itur* Rogers & Veale
wherof:

---

[41] Notwithstanding that one of the items below begins with 'In primis', the brackets show that the Boyle-Fystar obit begins one entry earlier.
[42] The caption is on folio 6v. but is linked by a bracket in the left hand margin to the first item in this section.
[43] Although missing through tearing, the valuation is the balancing figure of 30s.
[44] Possibly dittography.

Payd for chef rent to the comon rent of the Dene & Chapyter by
yere paying oute of the same howse iiiis. p:

exon*eratur* *per* eosd*em* Rogers & Veale

And so reman*s* xviiis. p:

[6n] [*Th]e Obytt fou*n*ded [***] ?mes

It*em* a c*er*ten medowe & land*es* lying in the p*a*ryshe of Madley in the countye of Her*eford* in the tenure of Will*ia*m ap R*ee*s and pay*e*the yerely [45] xs.

vend*itur* Tho*me* Hungate & Sim*oni* Aynesworth

It*em* the annuall rent out of the benefyce of Cellack in the sayd countye and pay*e*th yerely xxs.

[*Total*] xxxs.

Hereford Cathedral: an Obit

[6o] [*Obit] [***] [46]

It*em* a c*er*ten past*ure* & medo lying in the Suburbes of [*th]e cytye of Her*eford* w*i*th*out* Saynt Owens Gate in the tenure [*of] [*O]wen Gryffi*th* and paythe yerely xvis. p:

vend*itur* d*ic*tis Hungate & Aynesworth

wherof: [*Reprises]

[***] out of the same to ye p*re*bent of Bassham [47] yerely iiiis.

[***] [*o]ut of ye same to ye p*re*bent of ~~Wugne~~ Vyne [48] yerely iiiis.

[*Total reprises*] viiis.

exon*eratur* *per* eosdem

[*And so] reman*s* viiis. p:

Hereford Cathedral: Richard Jackson and Walter Negent's Obit

[f.7]**[6p]** The Obytte founded by Rychard Jackson & Walter Negent in the seyd Cath*edral* Churche

It*em* a c*er*ten medowe lying in Byford in the seyd county in the tenure of Rychard Warmecombe & pay*e*th yerely ixs.

It*em* c*er*ten other land*es* lying in Byford aforseyd in the tenure of Rychard Smythe and pay*e*th yerely vis.

It*em* a c*er*ten pece of wast ground lying in the back syde of the Bothhall in the Cytye of Her*eford* in the tenure of the Chamburlens of the same cytye & payd by S*ir* Thomas Clyburye clerke xs. e:

vend*itur* Jac:[*obo*] Rogers & Veale

[*Total*] xxvs.

Hereford Cathedral: Obit of Peter Acquablanca and Giles of Brusa

[6q] The Obytt fo*u*nded by Pet*er* Aquablanck & Gylys of Brusa in the seyd Cath*edral* Church

It*em* c*er*ten land*es* lying in Colwall in the ~~cytye~~ countie of Her*eford* in the tenure of Rob*er*t Cluterboke letten to hym by indenture xviis.

It*em* c*er*ten land*es* lying in Whythynton in the seyd countye in the tenure of Rychard Deme and pa*i*the yerely ixs. iiiid.

[*Total*] xxvis. iiiid. p:

Hereford Cathedral: Lady of Kilpeck's Obit

[6r] The Obyt founded by the Ladye of Kelpek in the sayd Churche

It*em* the annuall rent out of ye p*ar*sonage of Ludwardyn in the sayd countye late in the tenure of Rychard Warmecombe deceassed xls. e:

---

[45] Described only as 'an anniversary' in Hereford cathedral in the Patent Rolls (*CPR, 3 Edw. VI*, vii, 25).

[46] Anniversary founded by Robert Grendour, (*CPR, iii, 25*).

[47] Bartesham prebend.

[48] Eigne prebend.

Hereford Cathedral: Walter Decon's Obit

[6s] The Obyt of Walt*er* Decon founded in the sayd Cathedrall Churche of Hereff*ord*
Item the annuall rent going out of comon rent be longyng to
the Dean & Canons of the seyd cath*edral* Church iis. iiiid. e:

Hereford Cathedral: Maurice Newton and William Bentloyd's Obit

[6t] The Obyt founded by Morrys Newton & Will*iam* Bentloyd in the sayd Cath*edral* Churche
Item a c*er*ten ten*emen*te w*ith* thapp*er*ten*au*nces lying in the
p*ar*yshe of All Payntes in the Cytye of Hereford in the tenure
of Thomas Gybbons & Rob*ert* Glov*er* & payeth yere[ly*] [***] [49]
Item a garden lying by the towne dyche of [*Hereford] [50] in the tenure
of Robert Belcher and payth [***]
[*Reprises] [51]
Payd to the kynges ^ baylys ther [^] oute of the ten*emente* [***]
And also to the kynges ^ baylis ther [^] oute of the g[***] [***]
And so remayneth [***]
no*tatur* quo iure sol*vitur* d*om*ino Regi ballivo Civ*itatis*

Hereford Cathedral: Peter Solers, Thomas Folyat and Walter Pembridge's Obit

[f.7v] **[6u]** The Obytt founded by Peter Solers, Thomas Folyat , Walter ? Pemburge in the forseyd Churche
Item the annuall rent goyng out of the comon ^ rent [^] belongyng
to the Dean & Canons xiis.
Item the ann*u*all rent out of thalmes halle p*er*teynyng to the
tresorer of the same churche xs.
Item a ten*emen*te belongyng to the same obytte lying in the
p*ar*ysshe of All Saynt*es* in the sayd Cytye in the tenure of
Marye Free & pay*e*the yerely iis. viiid.
Item ii stables lying in the sayd p*ar*ysshe of All Saynt*es* in
the tenure of John Maland Walt*er* Nott & Thomas Benett ,
vi*delicet* ev*er*y stable iis. vis. e:
vend*itur* Rogers & Veale [52]
Item a cotage to the same stables adyoynyng in the tenure of
Syble Hatmaker and payeth yerely vis. viiid. e:
vend*itur* Rogers & Veale
[*Total*] xxxviis. iiiid.
wherof: Rep*r*ises [53]
Payd owte of the seyd stables ten*emen*te & cotage for chefe rent
unto the comon rent of the Den*e* & ~~cannons~~ Chapiter yerely iiis. iiiid. e:
exon*eratur per* eosd*em* Roge*r*s & Veale
And so remayneth xxxiiiis. p:

Hereford Cathedral: Richard Adkys and Others' Obit

[6v] The Obyt founded [***] [*Ry]chard Adkys [***] [*Ha]ll
Item the annuall rent goyng out of the chaunt*ery* of S. George in
the seyd Cath*edra*l Church*e* of Hereff*o*rd ~~xiiis. iiiid~~.
N*ichi*l *quia* on*eratur* infra s*er*vitiam de cantar*ia* ib*idem* iiii £. xiiis. iiiid. [6]
Item a c*er*ten ten*emen*te w*ith* thapp*er*ten*au*nces lying in the
p*ar*ysshe of Saynt Peters in the seyd Cytye in the tenure of
[*T]homas Harvye and pay*e*th yerely vis. viiid. e: p:

---

[49] Sold to Hungate and Aynesworth, (*CPR, iii, 25*).
[50] See *CPR, iii, 158.*
[51] There was probably no caption but a marginal total for reprises. It makes matters clearer for editorial purposes to suppose an implied caption.
[52] This and the next item sold to Rogers and Veale and linked by a bracket but in this edition the note is repeated.
[53] In the right hand margin.
[6] The precise positioning of the figures in this marginal note is hard to determine.

wherof: [*Reprises]
[*Pai]d oute of the same to Sir John Pryce knyght yerly iis.
[*A]lso payd to the almes halle appropryat to [***]or of the same cathedrall churche xiid.
[*Total*] iiis. p:
[***] Remayneth ~~xviis.~~ iiis. viiid. e:

Hereford Cathedral: John Comber's Obit

[f.8] **[6w]** The Obytte founded by John Comber in the seyd Churche
Item the annuall rent of c*er*ten land lying in Suburbes of ye seyd Cytye of Her*eford* belongyng to the vycars of ye quyer in ye ten*ure* of Thomas Wylcokkes by hynd Wye xxs. e:. p:

Hereford Cathedral: Richard Swynford and Nicholas Penitence's Obit

[6x] The Obytte founded by Rychard Swynford & Nicol Penytence in the sayd Cath*edra*l Church of Herefford
Item the annuall rent going out of ye p*ar*sonage of Dudlybury wi*th*in the ~~cyte~~ countie of Salop app*ropri*at to ye Den*e* & chapyter of ye the cath*edral* church of Her*eford* ~~and paythe to the clavengers of the same churche~~[54] Lxs.
Item the ann*u*all rent goyng out of the land*es* & farm of Burton in Hom Lacy the same ys in ye ten*ure* of John Skydmor esq[uy]er belo*n*gyng to the same Den*e* & Can*n*ons xls.
Item the ann*u*all rent going out of ye p*ar*sonage of Lugwardyn in the co*u*nty of Her*eford* in the tenour of Rychard Warmecombe esquyer xls.
[*Total*] vii £. p:

Hereford Cathedral: Peter Northampton's Obit

[6y] The Obyte founded by Peter Northampto*n* in the sayd Church
Item the ann*u*all rent out of a ten*emen*te lying in the Cyt*ie* of Her*eford* in the teno*ur* of John Boyle ~~ye seyd John have wi*th*drawn the seyd ann*u*all for c*er*ten yeres~~ vs. p:
John Boyle

Hereford Cathedral: Richard of Little Hereford's Obit

[6z] The Obyte founded by Ryc*hard* of Lyt*t*le Her*eford* in the sayd Cath*edral* Church
Item the annuall rent out of ii shoppes lying in the sayd Cyt*ie* in the tenure of John Bagott yerely vs. e:

Hereford Cathedral: Geoffrey Penitence's Obit

[6za] The Obyt founded by Geyffrey Penytence in the sayd Churche
Item the ann*u*all rent going out of ii yardes of land lying in Ov*er* Sapye in the co*u*ntey of Her*eford* in the tenour of Ric*hard* Barne ~~w*hi*ch hath wi*th*drawn the seyd rent c*er*ten~~ yeres viiis. e:

Hereford Cathedral: Harry Catchpole and Robert Gloucester's Obit

[6zb] The Obyte founded [by] Harry Cechepole & Rob*ert* Glocest*er* in the seyd Cath*edral* Churche
Item on*e* cotage lying in Myl*l*e Lane in the seyd Cytye in the tenure of John ap Thomas iiis.
Item a nother cotage lying in the same place in ye seyd Cyt*ie* in the tenure of Thomas Kent & pay*e*th yerely vs.
[*Total*] viiis. p:
wherof
Payd out of the seyd cotage to the Byshop of Hereford iiis. iiiid. p:
And so remayn*s* iiiis. viiid. p:

[54] A clavenger could be a mace-bearer or a key-keeper; in this case it is probably the latter, that is, the treasurer.

Hereford Cathedral: James Barkley and Walter Carles's Obit

[f.8v] **[6zc]** The Obyt founded by James Barkley & Walt*er* Carles in the seyd Churche
Item the ann*u*all re*n*t going out of a close lying in Home Lacye called Bugges Close in ye tenure of Will*ia*m Caldycot yer*e*ly iis. e:
Item out of c*er*ten land*es* lying in Hom*e* Lacy called Deyes land*es* in the ten*ure* of the seyd Will*ia*m yerely xiid. e:
Item out of a garden lying in the same town in ye tenure of Thomas Andrewes yerely iiiid. e:
vend*itur* Jo:[*hanni*] Cupp*er*[55]
Item oute of *cer*ten land*es* lying in the same town in the tenure of Wyllyam Barrell yerely ixd. e:
[Total] iiiis. id. p: e:
vend*itur* Joh:[*hanni*] Cupper & Ric*ardo* Traver

Hereford Cathedral: Richard of St. Albans's Obit

[6zd] The Obyte founded by Ric*hard* of Saynt Albons in the seyd Churche
I*tem* a ten*emen*te lying [in] Weston ^ upon Fromey [^] in the countey of Her*eford* in the tenure of Edward Smyth & pay*e*th yerely for the same vs. e:

Hereford Cathedral: John Foster's Obit

[6ze] The Obyte fo*und*e*d* by John Foster in the sayd Cath*edral* Churche of Her*eford*
Item the ann*u*all rent going out of *cer*ten land*es* in Wollhope in the tenure of Kat*e*ryn Hylle wedowe[56] ~~vis. iiiid.~~ ~~iiiid.~~ iiiid. e:
Item oute of the land*es* in the tenure of Thom*as* Wheler iid. ob. e:
Item the ann*u*all rent out of c*er*ten land*es* in the tenour off Harry Herdyberd yerely iiiid. e:
Item the annuall rent oute of *cer*ten land*es* in the tenure of Thomas Wheler yerely iiid. e:
Item the ann*u*all rent out of c*er*ten land*es* in the tenure of Walt*er* Stallard yerely iiid. e:
Item oute of certen landes in the tenure of Walt*er* Turnor yerely vid. e:
[f.9] Item oute of c*er*ten land in ye tenure of Thom*as* Love yerly iid. e:
Item oute of *cer*ten land in ye tenour of John Wynt*er* yerly iiiid. e:
Item oute of *cer*ten land*es* late in the tenour of Rob*ert* Love yerly iiiid. e:
Item oute of a howse called O*ur* Lady Howse yerely iid. e:[57]
[*Total*] ~~vs.~~ ~~xd. ob.~~ iis. xd. ob. p:
Totu*m* vend*itur* Reve & Johnson ac al*ii*[58]

Hereford Cathedral: Simon Cartbridge's Obit

[6zf] The Obytte founded by Symond Cartbrydge in the sayd Churche
Item the annuall rent goyng out of c*er*ten landes lying in Clehunger in the countye of Hereff*ord* in the tenure of the vycare of Clehunger yerely e: p: iiiis.
No*tatu*r This lande is the K*inge*s ex informa*tione* M*aiori*s Hereff*ordiensis*

Hereford Cathedral Totals

[6zg] Sum total of the forsaid obittes the reprises not deducted: xxxviii £. ~~ix~~ vis. xid.
Reprises yerely ~~xxxis. iid~~. xxviis. iid.
And so remayn*s* clere xxxvi £. ~~xixs~~. ~~xls~~. .. xixs. ixd. p: e:[59]

55 This and the previous two items are joined by a bracket with one marginal note: 'sold to John Cupper'.
56 See section 53c.
57 At this point the original bracket linked to the obit total continues to encompass the figures for the next obit, but was later severed by placing two capital Ds where one bracket should have ended and the next begun.
58 This total and marginal note appear on the previous page but must include the first four items on this page. The 'alii' was probably Henry Herdson, skinner, of London, (*CPR, iii, 375*).
59 Although the loss of some figures makes it impossible to be sure, these totals appear to be the totals of sections 6b to 6zf inclusive (the obits of the canons and petty canons).

The Rent Roll of all Such Land*es* & Ten*ement*es as ap*er*teynyth to the Chauntrys founded in the P*ar*ysshe Churche of All Saynt*es* as here aft*er* apperethe by Order

All Saints, Hereford: Our Lady Chantry

[f.9v] 7 Fyrst the Rentall of All Land*es* & Ten*emen*tes belongyng to the Chaunt*ery* of O*u*r Lady in the seyd Church

In p*ri*mis on*e* ten*emen*te w*ith* a close in the tenure of Rychard James xlvis. p:
vend*itur* Th:[*ome*] Hungate & Sim:[*oni*] Aynesworthe

Item ii gardens in the tenure of Thomas Granger by yere xxis. viiid. e:
vend*itur* W:[*illelmo*] Britten & Ambrosi*o* Nicholus

Item on*e* ten*emen*te in the p*ar*ysshe of All Saynt*es* in the tenure of Edmond Shappe iis. e:
vend*itur* W:[*illelmo*] Britten & Ambrosi*o* Nicholus

Item on*e* Stable in the tenure of Marg*ar*ett P*er*kyns by yere iiiis.
vend*itur* Hungate & Aynesworthe
vend*itur per* nome*n* Ja:[*cob*i] Warnecombe

Item on*e* stable in the tenure of John Stephyns iiiis.
Item on*e* ten*emen*te in the tenure of Thomas Sadler iiiis.
Item on*e* ten*emen*te in the tenure of Lewys Hoper vis.
Item out of the ten*emen*te wherin Thom*as* Henbage do dwell xiid.
Item on*e* garden in the tenure of Phylyp Symond*es* iis. iiiid. e:
vend*itur* Tho:[*me*] Hungate & S:[*imoni*] Aynesworthe

Item on*e* pece of voyde ground in the tenure of the sayd Phelyppe iiiid.
vend*itur* W:[*illelmo*] Britten & Ambrosi*o* Nicholas

+Item on*e* ten*emen*te in the tenure of Rychard Baker vis.
+Item on*e* ten*emen*te in the tenure of Will*iam* Hughys xvis.
Item on*e* ten*emen*te in the tenour of Hughe Bagge ixs.
Item on*e* ten*emen*te in the tenour of John Tylar vs.
Item a stable w*ith* a garden in the tenure of John Partryg iiis. iiiid.
vend*itur* Rogers & Veale

Item on*e* ten*emen*te w*ith* a garden in the tenure of Hughe Welshe viiis. e:
vend*itur* Rogers & Veale

It*em* on*e* ten*emen*t wit*h* a garden in the tenure of Harry Tann*er* chaplayn iiiis. e:
vend*itur* eisd*em*

Item vi acres of errable land in the tenour of Walt*er* Nott ixs. e:
vend*itur* Tho:[me] Hungate & Simoni Aynesworthe

It*em* iiii acr*es* of errable land in ye tenure of Hugh Stuard vis. viiid.
vend*itur* Tho:[*me*] Hungate & Simoni Aynesworthe

Item on*e* pece of vacant ground in ye tenure of the same Hughe vid.
vend*itur* W:[*illelmo*] Britto*n* & Ambrossi*o* Nicholas

Item xiii acres of errable land in the tenure of Hughe Gybbons xxs. e:
vend*itur* eisd*em* Thome & Simoni

[*Total*] viii £. xviiis. xd. e:

wherof:

[f.10] Rep*ri*ses

In p*ri*mis to the kyng*es* bayly of the cytye of Her*eford* iiis. iiid. ob.
exon*eratur per* Hungate & Aynesworthe

Item to the Byshope of Herefford iis. ixd.
Item to the Deane & Chapyter iis.
Item to the p*re*bend of Ynge vs. viiid.
Item to the supp*re*ssed howse of Langtony ~~iis. viiid~~.
extinguit*ur* stet

Item to the comon backhowse xvid.
Item to the supp*re*sed howse of Dynmore iis.

[*Total reprises*] xixs. viiid. ob. p: [60]

Remanet clare vii £. xxid. ob. e: [61]

[60] The total is before deducting the struck through figure.

[61] There is an error here. The sub-totals are correct but the final net total should be £7 19s. 9½d. The error is not explained by the reinstatement of the figure of 2s. 8d. Perhaps it was badly copied from an anterior document showing 'xixs. id.' rather than 'xxid', as shown here.

All Saints, Hereford: The Holy Rood and S. James Chantry

8. The Rentroll of All the Landes & Ten*emen*tes app*er*teynyng to the Chaunt*ery* of The Roode & Seynt James w*ith*in the P*a*rysh above seyd

In p*ri*mis on*e* ten*emen*t in the tenure of Thom*as* Russhell xxs. +

no*tatur* ist*i* xxs. vend*itur* Joh*an*ni Butler & Hugoni P*ar*tridge

Item a ten*emen*te in the tenure of Rychard Davys baker xxis. iiiid. +

Item a ten*emen*t w*ith* thapp*er*tenaunces lying in the p*a*rysshe of Lydemuchgrosse ^ in the tenure of Thom*as* Baughe [^] xvs.

vend*itur* Jacobo Rogers & Ric*ardo* Veale

Item a c*er*ten medowe in the tenure of John Adys vis. viiid.

exon*eratur* q*uia* vend*itur* Hereford & Wilys*on*

Item oute of mess*uage* in the tenure of Will*iam* Goldsmyth viiis.

Item out of a ten*emen*te wherin ~~Rychard~~ Will*iam* Bowyer dwellyth iiis. iiiid.

Item on*e* pece of voyd ground in the tenure of John Chambyr iis. vid.

Item on*e* ten*emen*te in the tenure of Lewys Apryce xiid.

Item on*e* shop voyd in the p*a*ryshe of Saynt Peter iiiis.

Item An P*ar*tryge iiis.

Item of Roger Hyll iiiis.

Item of John Pyrry iiis.

Item of John Gytteyon iiis. iiiid.

Item of John Dune iiis.

Item of Elyzabeth ap Thomas iiiis.

Item of An Freman for a chambre [62] xxd.

Item of Margaret Carver for a chamb*re* xvid.

It*em* on*e* ten*emen*t w*ith* a garden in the tenure of a chant*ery* p*ri*est ^ther [^] <u>xvs.</u>

[*Total*] vi £. iid. p:

wherof

[f.10v] Rep*ri*ses to the Baylys of the said Citie

In p*ri*mis to the kyng*es* maiestye iiid.

Item to the kyng for a voyd ground xiid.

Item to the Bysshoppe iiiis.

Item to the Chaunt*ery* of O*ur* Ladye in the same Church ~~xiid.~~

nich*i*l q*uia* allocat*ur* in Cantaria p*redicte* B*eate* Marie ~~non hoc~~ & oner*atur* [63] in p*redicte* cant*aria*

Item to the Bysshoppe <u>iiiis.</u>

[*Total reprises*] ixs. iiid. p:

Remanet clar*e* Cxs. xid. e:

All Saints, Hereford: S. Anne's Chantry

9 The Rentall of All the Landes & Ten*emen*tes app*er*teynyn to ye Chaunt*er*ey of Saynt An w*ith*in the P*a*rysh Church aforseyd

In p*ri*mis a ten*emen*te in the tenure of Thom*as* Clem*en*t xlvis. viiid.

vend*itur* Tho:[*me*] Hungate & Simoni Aynesworthe [64]

~~Item the owte rent iiis. iiiid.~~

~~Item to the Deane & Chapyter xxiid.~~

~~Item to Goreld xviiid.~~

Item a ten*emen*te in the tenure of Ryc*hard* Apryce xxvis. viiid.

Item the oute rent to M*aste*r Pryce ~~iiis.~~

Item a bakhowse in the Worthall nowe voyde xxs.

Item *one* garden with a pygyon howse + e: viiis.

vend*itur* W:[*illelmo*] Britten & Ambros*io* Nicholas

Item the oute rent to the kynges bayly of the Cyty ~~xxd.~~

Item a garden w*ith* a closse + e: <u>vis.</u>

vend*itur* dict*is* Britten & Nicolas

---

[62] 'for a chambre' was added in a different handwriting, as was the note on the next entry.

[63] The only item valued at 12d. in the valuations of that chantry is the house of Thomas Henbage, but his name does not appear in this list.

[64] This marginal note is bracketed with the next four items.

[*Total*] Cviis. iiiid. [65]

wherof:

Item payd out of thes som*mes* aforsayd in the charge allowed p*arti*culerly ~~xis. iiid~~.

inde ixs. viiid. exon*eratur* per Hungate & Aynesworthe & xixd. resid*uum* eiusd*em* sum*me* exon*eratur per* dict*os* Britten & Nicholas

Reman*et* clar*e* iiii £. xvis. id. [66]

All Saints, Hereford: Trinity Chantry

[f.11] **10.** The Rentroll of all the Land*es* & Ten*ementes* app*er*teynyng to the Chaunt*ery* of the Blessyd Trynyte w*ith*in the P*ar*yssh Churche afor rehersed

In p*ri*mis one ten*emen*te in the tenure of Thom*as* Havard gentylman iiiis.

It*em* oute of the ten*emen*te of Mathowe Geffreys xviiis. vid.

It*em* one ten*emen*te in the tenure of Rob*er*t Glov*er* viiis.

It*em* Rychard Hosyer holdyth a burgage iis.

It*em* one ten*emen*te with ii gardens in the tenure of the inco*m*bent xiiis. iiiid. e:

It*em* on*e* other garden in the seyd incumbent*es* hand*es* xxd. e:

vend*itur* W:[*illelmo*] Brite*n* & Ambrosio Nicholas

It*em* a barne, a garden iiii acres di*medietas* of errable ground in the hand*es* of Rychard P*ar*tryg xis. e:

vend*itur* Ja:[*cobo*] Rogers & Ric*ard*o Veale

It*em* Will*ia*m Coyd holdyth on*e* ten*emen*te w*ith* ii cottes xiis.

It*em* John Taborer & Welshe John holdyth ii cotages viiis.

It*em* Edmond Stele holdyth ii ten*ementes* w*ith* vii gardens to them belongyng xxis.

It*em* Rob*er*t Davys holdyth on*e* voyde ground xvid.

It*em* John Marsh & John Sheward holdyth on*e* house, a shop w*ith* a garden vis.

It*em* Edmond Thryst holdyth on*e* ten*emen*te w*ith* a garden iiis.

It*em* a lytle howse w*ith* a garden yat ye seyd incu*m*bent have vs.

vend*itur* Will*elm*o Brytte*n* & Ambrosio Nicholas

It*em* Thomas Stok*es* holdythe a voyd ground xiid.

[*Total*] Cxv~~i~~s. xd. [67] p:

wherof: Rep*ri*ses

In p*ri*mis to the kyng*es* maieste ^baylis ther [^] for cheffe rent iiiis. iid.

It*em* to the Bysshope of Heref*ord* iis.

It*em* to the Gorrall fee vid.

It*em* to the De*a*ne & Chapyter xiid.

~~It*em* for the sayd Incumbent*es* tenthes xis. iid.~~

[*Total reprises*] viis. viiid. p:

Reman*et* clare Cviiis. iid. e:

All Saints, Hereford: Obits and Lights

[f.11v] **11.** The Rentroll of All the Land*es* & Ten*ementes* belongyng to the Menten*a*unce of Obytt*es* & Lyght*es* in the P*ar*yshe of All Saynt*es* w*ith*in the Cytye of Herefford

In p*ri*mis Morgan Ogan holdyth a close belongyng to the Obytte called P*ar*sons Obytte iiis. viiid. e:

vend*itur* W:[*illelmo*] Britten & Ambros*io* Nicholas

It*em* John Roboroghe holdyth on*e* ten*emen*te w*ith* a garden app*er*taynyng to Hugh VaZhans Obytte xviiis.

It*em* John Maylard, Rob*er*t ap Howell, Mathow Jeffres holdyth thre shoppes to the fyndyng of an obytte called Wyghtfyld Obytte ~~& certen lyghtes~~ xxs.

[*Total*] xlis. viiid. p:

---

[65] This the total after striking out the 5 items above.

[66] This the total before striking out the deduction of 11s. 3d. above.

[67] The total is £5 15s. 10d. after striking through an 'i',

wherof: Rep*ri*ses
In p*ri*mis oute of the ten*emen*t of John Roboroghe for a cheffe rent to the Bysshopp of Herefford iis. vid.
It*em* oute of the same house to the church work*e*s of All Halous vid.
It*em* oute of the sayd iii shoppes for the chefe rent to the kyng*e*s baylys ther iiiid.
[*Total reprises*] iiis. iiiid. p:
Remanet clare xxxviiis. iiiid. e:

St. Owen's, Hereford: Our Lady Chantry

12. The Rentall of all ye Land*e*s & Ten*emen*t*e*s belongyng to the Chant*ery* of O*ur* Lady within the p*ar*ysh of Saynt Owens
In p*ri*mis a garden in the tenure of Ryc*hard* Sandy vs. n*ichi*l
It*em* S*ir* Thomas Pember holdyth one garden iis. n*ichi*l
It*em* the same S*ir* Thomas holdyth on*e* other garden iis. n*ichi*l
It*em* John Nashe holdyth on*e* ten*emen*te viis.
It*em* John Chance holdyth a ten*emen*te vs.
It*em* John Spycer for on*e* ten*emen*te vis. n*ichi*l
It*em* Will*ia*m Barcley for on*e* garden iis.
+It*em* Hughe Adams for a voyd ~~grounde~~ garden xiid.
[f.12] It*em* Thomas Marten a ten*emen*te xvis.
It*em* Morice ap Howell a ten*emen*te xxs.
It*em* Harry Dudeston for a garden vis. viiid.
n*ichi*l [68]
It*em* Thomas Stok*e*s for a garden vis. viiid.
+It*em* Edward ^ Foreste [^] barbor a garden & a chamber vis. viiid.
vend*itur* Tho:[*me*] Reve & al*io*
omitte this
It*em* Hugh Walsh for a ten*emen*te xiid.
It*em* Mistres Harvard a ten*emen*te xviiid.
It*em* Gryffyt ap Howell a ten*emen*te vid.
It*em* Thom*as* Scarlett a ten*emen*te xiid.
It*em* John Skyrme a ten*emen*te xiid.
It*em* M*aste*r Warmecombe a ten*emen*te xiid.
It*em* a ten*emen*te of theyres of Roger More xviiid.
[*Total*] iiii £. xiiis. vid. [69] p:
wherof: Rep*ri*ses
In p*ri*mis ~~out of~~ ^ to [^] the p*re*bend of Barssham xiiis. iiiid.
It*em* to S*ir* John Aprece knyght xxiiid.
It*em* to the kyng*e*s bayly iiiid. ob.
It*em* to the Deane & Chapytur iiis. iiiid.
[*Total reprises*] xviiis. xid. ob. p:
Remanet clar*e* Lxxiiiis. vid. ob. e:

1. 8. 4.	4. 13. 6.	4. 6. 10.	4. 13. 6.
1. 2. 0.	6. 8.	3. 9. 4.	2. 9. 4.
	4. 6. 10.	17. 6.	2. 4. 2.
	1. 8. 4.		
	2. 18. 6		
	2. 0. 0.		
			18. 6. [70]

[68] This item and the next each have the abbreviated word 'nichil' written against them in both left and right hand margins.
[69] This is the total having no regard to the marginal notations of 'nichil' and 'omytte this'.
[70] This is arithmetic with 'pounds, shillings and pence'. Although some of these figures can be reconstructed from the valuation-lists above, there seems to be no consistency and their significance escapes the present editor.

St. Owen's, Hereford: Trinity Chantry

[f.12v] **13**. The Rentall of all the Land*es* & Tene*men*tes belongyng to the Chant*er*y of the Holy Trynyte w*ith*in the P*ar*yshe Church of Saynt Owens w*ith*in the Cytye of Herefo*rd*

In p*ri*mis a ten*emen*te in the tenure of Rychard Baker	iiiis.
+ It*em* a ten*emen*te in the tenure of Wyllyam Yatton	vis. viiid.
Item a ten*emen*te in the tenure of Lewys Aprece	vis.
It*em* a ten*emen*te in the tenure of M*istre*s Alys Scull n*ichi*l	iiis. viiid.
+ Item a gardyng w*ith*out Seynt Owens Gate	iiis. iiiid.
Item ann*u*yte owte of the land*es* lying voide in the Cabag*e* Lane in the tenure of Edward Crasset	xiid.
[*Tota*l]	xxiiiis. viiid. p:

wherof: Resolut*es*

In p*ri*mis payd ^ to the Kynges baylis there [^] oute of a ten*emen*te in the tenou*r* of Rychard Baker	vid.
Item p*ai*d oute of a ten*emen*te to S*ir* John Appryce	xxd.
Item payd out of a ten*emen*te of Lewys Apprece to the ^ Canons bayly [^]	xiiiid.
Item p*ai*d oute of a ten*emen*te of M*istre*s Scull to the kyng*es* bayly ^ther [^]	iiis.
Item p*ai*d oute of a garden at Seint Owens Gate to the kyng*es* bayly	iis.
[*Total reprises*]	viiis. iiiid. p:
Reman*et* clar*e*	xvis. iiiid. e:

St. Nicholas, Hereford: Obits

14. The Rentroll*e* of all the Land*es* & Ten*emen*tes belongyng to the Meinten*a*unce of Obyttes & Land*es* [71] w*ith*in the P*a*ryshe of Saynt Nicol

In p*ri*mis John Smyth holdyth one close	iis. vd.
Item on*e* ten*emen*te in the tenure of Walt*er* Phelyp	xs. viiid.
Item on*e* ten*emen*te in the tenure of John Keryke	iis. id.
Item out of the howse of Hughe Taylor toward ye lampe	iis.
[*Total*]	xviis. iid. [72] p:

Rep*ri*ses

In p*ri*mis to the Busshop of Hereford	iiiid.
Item to the Deane & Chapyter	vd.
[*Total reprises*]	ixd. p:

no*tatur* istud vd. exon*eratur per* eosdem Reve & Johnson:
[***]te ten*ementum* in te*nura* Walteri Phelippe ?ac
[***] xs. viiid. ^ *per* ann*um* [^] p*arcel*l*um* sum*me*
xviis. iid. vend*itur* [***] Reve & Johnson p*er* nomen
Joh*ann*is Edwardes [***] & Johnes Furrat al*ias* Gonnar

Remanet clar*e*	xvis. vd.

St. Nicholas, Hereford: Our Lady Chantry

[f.13] **15**. The Rentroll of All the Land*es* & Ten*emen*t*es* belongyng to O*u*r Lady Chaunt*er*ey in Saynt Nycolas P*ar*yshe

In p*ri*mis of the P*ri*or of Langtonye		Ls.
Item of Willyam Smothye		viiis.
Item an annuall rent going out of ye land*es* of Maskall cancell*atur* quom*in*usq*ue* melius ex*aminatur*		? ~~xixs.~~ [73]
Item of Thomas Hattmaker vend*itur* Jo:[*hanni*] Butler & Partridge		viiis.
+ Item of John Taylor at Kyng*es* Dyche		viiis. +
Item of John Phelyp*es* for thre ten*emen*t*es*	~~xiiiis. iiiid.~~	xiiis. iiiid.
Item of Laurence Walker for on*e* ten*emen*te		xs.

[71] It seems likely that 'Lights' was intended rather than 'Lands'.
[72] An auditor's use grid shows this figure.
[73] This line was written in after the next line had been written. See section 53c.

Item of Wyllyam Barne for one ten*emen*te iiis.
Item on*e* ten*emen*te nyghe to S. Nycolas churche ^ in Blak Lane [^] iiiis.
Item one ten*emen*te lying in ~~the Lane land~~ ^ Worthe Lane [^] iiiis.
+ Item a garden in the tenure of Walt*er* Marshe iis.
+ Item on*e* other garden viiid.
Item on*e* garden ~~by hind Wye~~ iis.
Item a ten*emen*t by Seynt Nicholas Church vis. viiid.
Item out of a tenement lying at Wyebridg called Vyggers by yere iis.[74]

[*Total*] ~~vi £. ixs. viiid.~~ ~~vi £. xxd.~~ vi £. ~~iis. iiid.~~ xxd.

vi £. xxd. no*tatu*r there is viiis. p*ar*cell of this som*me* of vi £. xxd. for a ten*emen*t in the use of Tho:[*mas*] Russell[75] graunted to Joh*ann*i Butler & Hugoni P*ar*tridge & there is no suche in and here exp*ressed* Ideo &c ?nihil.

Rep*ri*ses
In p*ri*mis to the kyng*es* baylys there xxd.
Item to the Cannons of Here*ford* iis. vid.
Item to the Lord of Saynt Jones vid.
Item to ~~the pryce~~[76] M*aste*r Pryce of Here*ford* iiiid.
Item to the Lord of ~~Urmond~~ Urlmond[77] xviiid.
Item to the kyng*es* maieste for Langtony extinguit*ur* ~~xiid.~~

[*Total reprises*] viis. vid.[78] p:

Reman*et* clar*e* ~~Cxiiis. iid.~~ ~~vi £. iiis. xd.~~ Cxiiis. iid. p: e:

St. Martin's, Hereford: Our Lady Chantry

16. The Rentrol of All the Land*es* & Ten*emen*t*es* belongyng to ye Chaunt*ery* of O*ur* Lady w*ith*in ye P*ar*ysh of S. M*ar*tens
In p*ri*mis the chaunt*ery* house w*ith* a garden therto belongyng xiis.
vend*itur* Tho*me* M*ar*she & Roger*o* Will*iam*z
Item Rob*er*t Godman holdyth a howse xs. iiid.
Item a house in the tenure of John Kerry iiiis.
+It*em* Fowke Leyghton holdyth iii acres of errable land & on*e* close vis. viiid.
+Item on*e* house in the tenure of Will*iam* Glov*er* viiis.
Item on*e* ten*emen*te in the tenure of John Taylor vis. viiid.
nich*i*l
[f.13v] Item a howse w*ith* a barn & a garden in ye tenour of Robart Carwyn vis. viiid.
It*em* a c*er*ten errable land in the tenure of John Ken*er*sley vis. iid. ob.
It*em* c*er*ten errable land in the tenure of Will*iam* Howell xiis.
It*em* one garden & a house in the tenure of Thom*as* a Powell iiis.
It*em* one other garden in the occupying of the seyd chaunt*er*ey p*ri*est vis. vid.
Item a howse in the tenure of John Spens*er* w*ith* a garden vis. viiid.
n*ichi*l

[*Total*] iiii £. viiis. viid. ob. p: e:

wherof: Rep*ri*ses
In p*ri*mis to M*aste*r Prece for a cheffe rent iiiis.
Item to M*aste*r Rychard Berowe for a chef rent iiis.
~~Item to the Deane & Chapytur iis. iiid.~~
Item to the Tresurer xiid.
Item to the Howse of Akenburye vid.
Item p*ai*d to the kyng*es* maieste xviid.
Item payd to the kyng*es* maieste vid.
Item to the vicars of the Cathedrall Churche of Herefford xiid.

[*Total reprises*] ~~xiiis. viid.~~[79] xis. ~~iiiid.~~ vd.

Reman*et* clar*e* ~~Lxxs. ob.~~ e: p: Lxxviis. iid. ob.

---

[74] This line was written in afterwards in a different hand.
[75] Thomas Russell was presumably also known as Thomas Hattmaker.
[76] This mistake suggests that this document may have been copied from one or more antecedent documents.
[77] Unidentified but more likely to be a 'lord of a manor' than a title of nobility.
[78] The total is before the the striking out of the final item.
[79] The total before the cancelled 2s. 3d. is 13s 8d. and, after the deduction, became 11s. 5d.

~~*Memorandum* that thys som*me* of xiis. ys charged in the totall som*me* for that Will*iam* Crowche esquyer hath purchased the same of the kyng*es* Ma*ie*ste~~

~~*notatur* unde rat*ione* *litt*ere paten*tis* de p*er*quis*itione* redd*ent* xiis.~~

? St. Martin's, Hereford: Obits

17.	Obyttes	
	Item out of the ten*emen*t of Thom*as* A More to the fyndyng of one obytte	iis. vid.
	Item out of ye ten*emen*t of Thom*as* Webbe for one obytte	iis. vid.
	[*Total*]	vs. p:

St. Peter's, Hereford: St.John the Baptist's Chantry

[f.14] **18.**	The Rentroll of All the Land*es* & Ten*emen*t*es* belongyng to the Chaunt*ery* of S. John Baptyst w*ith*in the p*ar*ysh Church of Saynt Peturs	
	In p*ri*mis on*e* ten*emen*te in the tenure of Thom*as* M*ar*she	iiiis. vid.
	Item on*e* ten*emen*te in the tenure of Rychard Go*u*ghe	iiiis. vid.
	Item a garden in the tenure of Thomas More	viiis.
	+It*em* a garden in the tenure of Thomas Hayvard	viiis. +
	It*em* on*e* oth*er* garden in the tenure of Harry Dudeston	vs. iiid.
	+Item ii stables ii gardens in ye tenour of Thom*as* Church	viis. iiiid. +
	+Item on*e* ten*emen*te in the tenure of Phelyp Lucas	viiis. +
	Item on*e* ten*emen*te in the tenure of Harry Brace	iiiis.
	Item for the halfe on*e* garden in ye tenure of Ric*hard* Church	xiid.
	Item on*e* garden in the tenure of James Badham	iii~~i~~s. iiiid.
	Item for on*e* shop in the tenure of Thom*as* Gybbons	iis.
	vend*itur* W:[*illelmo*] Britten & Ambros*io* Nicholas	
	[*Total*]	Lvs. xid. [80] p:
	wherof: Rep*r*ises	
	In p*ri*mis payd to the kyng*es* maieste	vid.
	Item p*ai*d to the kyng*es* maieste	vid.
	Item p*ai*d to the kyng*es* maieste	xiid.
	Item to the Dene & Chapyter of Herefford	xiid.
	[*Total reprises*]	iiis. p:
	Remanet clare	Liis. xid. e:

19.	The Rentroll of All the Land*es* & Ten*emen*t*es* belo*n*gyng to O*u*r Lady Chaunt*ery* in the p*ar*ysh Church of S. Peters	
	In p*ri*mis a chamber late in the tenure of Will*iam* Gybbys nu*n*c vacat*a*	iiis. iiiid. +
	Item on*e* other chamber wherin the p*ri*est lyeth	iis. +
	Item a chamber in the tenure of S*ir* Dav*i*d Mey	iis. viiid. +
	Item a cotage in the tenure of John Trulove	iis. +
	Item a cotage in the tenure of Margrett Hyggys	iis. +
	Item a messuage next adioynyng to the same	iis. ~~viiid.~~ +
	Item a cotage voyd	vis. viiid.+
	Item a cotage in the tenure of Elzabeth Tayler	vs. +
	Item a stable in the tenure of M*aste*r Blackeston	iiis. iiiid. +
	Item one stable in the tenure of Thomas Bayly	iiis. iiiid. +
[f.14v]	Item a garden in the tenure of John Smythe	xxd.
	Item a garden in the tenure of Thomas Clement	xxd.
	n*ichi*l	
	+Item on*e* garden & a ten*emen*te in ye tenure of Edward Colles	vs. +
	Item on*e* ten*emen*te & a stable in the tenour of Phelyp Walt*er*	vs.
	vend*itur* R:[*icardo*] Venables & Jo:[*hanni*] Maynard	
	+Item a ten*emen*t & a garden in the tenure of Ryc*hard* Sandye	iiiis. +
	Item a ten*emen*te in the tenure of Hugh ap Rychard	xiiis. iiiid.
	Item ii tenementes in the tenure of John Bryan	xxvis.
	Item a stable & a garden in the tenure of Thom*as* Gyttyns	vs.

[80] Less the correction to the penultimate item.

Item a ~~?mes~~ a ten*emen*te in the tenure of Will*ia*m Smothye xs.
Item a garden in the tenure of Rychard ap Res iis.
n*ichi*l
It*em* a barn w*ith* a garden in the tenure of John Wyllmottes vs. iiiid.
Item on*e* other garden in the tenure of Glyn Jenkyns xviiid.
vend*itur* Venables & Jo:[*hanni*] Maynard
It*em* a shoppe late in the tenure of John Clarke now voyd iis.
[*Total*] Cxiiiis. xd. p:

wherof: Rep*ri*ses
In p*ri*mis to the kyng*e*s maieste iiis. viiid.
It*em* to Sir John A Prece knyght iiiis.
It*em* to the Dean & Chapyter of Herefford viis. iid.
Item Will*ia*m Gower for the barn of Burford iiiis.
[*Total reprises*] xviiis. xd. p:
Remanet clare iiii £. xvis. e:

St. Peter's, Hereford: Trinity Chantry

20. The Rentall of All the Land*e*s & Ten*emen*tes belongyng to the Chaunt*er*ey of the Holy Blessed Trynyte w*ith*in the P*ar*ysh Church aforseyd
In p*ri*mis a ten*emen*te in the tenure of Hugh Rawlynges xls. +
Item a ten*emen*te in the tenure of Kateryne Treamor xls.
It*em* a ten*emen*te in the tenure of John Seward xls. +
vend*itur* Rogers & Veale
Item a ten*emen*te in the tenure of John Brayne xxvis. viiid.
Item a ten*emen*te in the tenure of John Ecley vis. viiid.
Item a garden in the tenure of Sir D*av*id Mey iis. e:
vend*itur* Rogers & Veale
[*Total*] vii £. xvs. iiiid. p:
wherof
n*otatu*r ~~xls.~~ tene*mentu*m in tenura Katerine Treamor ad xls. *per* ann*um* con*cessa* Tho:[*me*] Reve & Johnson et al*iis* et exoneratur iiiis. vid. eisdem alloc*atur* in perquis*itionibu*s eiusd*em* vi*delice*t xiid. maior*i* et ball*ivo* Civitatis Herfford*iensis* & iiis. vid. [***] decan*o* & capit*ulo*

[f.15] Rep*ri*ses
In p*ri*mis to the kyng*e*s maieste iiis. iiid.
exon*eratur per* Reve & Johnson
It*em* to the Deane & ~~Chapyter~~ Canons iiis. vid.
exon*eratur per* Rogers & Veale
Item ^ to [^] S*ir* John A Prece knyght xviiid.
exon*eratur per* eosd*em* Rogers & Veale
[*Total reprises*] viiis. iiid. p:
Remanet clare vii £. viis. id. e:

St. Peter's, Hereford: Mary Magdalen Chantry

21. The Rentall of All the Land*e*s & Ten*emen*tes belongyng to the Cha*unte*ry of [^] Bless*ed* [^] Mary Magdelen in the P*ar*yshe of S. Pet*er* .
In p*ri*mis a ten*emen*te in the tenure of Rychard P*ar*tryg Liiiis. xd. p:
N*otatu*r the Liiiis. xd. in the tenure of Richarde P*ar*trig in the P*ar*ticlers made unto Hungate & Aynesworth {+++} but Liiis. iiiid. by the copye of the particlers dothe appere ?and also the somme of Lxxis. vid. [+++] [81] but Lxs. &c Ideo ?n*ihi*l [82]
Item on*e* ten*emen*te in the tenure of John Will*ia*m barbor Lxxis. vid. e:
vend*itur*

[81] In this marginal note there are two places where the words are untranscribed here. The meaning is unknown but it is the same word in each case.
[82] This marginal note has been squeezed between section s 20 and 21, but relates to the first and second items in the latter section, so as been moved there in this edition. The meaning is unclear.

Item a ferme in the tenure of John Wyllyams xxiis. iiiid. e:
Item a voyd grounde in the paryshe of All Sayntes xviiis. vid. e:

venditur
Notatur totalis cantaria ultra xviiis. vid. venditur
Tho:[me] Hungate & Simoni Aynesworth &
xviiis. vid. venditur Jacobo Rogers & Ricardo Veale [83]

[Total] viii £. viis. iid. [84] p:

wherof: Reprises
In primis Rychard Partryg payeth to the kynges maieste xviiid. e:
Item John Wyllyams payeth to the kynges Grace for a quyt rent xviiid. e:
Item John Wyllyams payeth to John Warden xs. e:
Item the seyd John Wyllyams payeth out of hys ferm iiiis. iiiid. e:
Item the voyd grounde payeth to the Dene & Chapyter iis. vid. e:

exoneratur Rogers
Item the seyd voyd grounde vacat rent ~~xvis.~~

exoneratur per perquisitores
[Total reprises] ~~xxxvs.~~ xixs. ~~xd.~~ [85] p:

Remanet clare vii £. viis. ~~xd.~~ iiiid. e:

St. Peter's, Hereford: William Kenchester's Anniversary

22. The Paryshe Churche of S. Peters within the Cyty of Hereford
Item one tenemente with a garden lying in the Cytye of Hereford in a strete ther called Bystrete nowe in the tenure of Rychard Sandy was gevyn to the vycary of the seyd parysh for ever to fynd & menteyn one anyversary for ever for the soule of William Kenchester iiis. iiiid. + e:

City of Hereford Totals

[23] Totalis Lxix £. xiiis. viiid. [...]
Summe total of all the chauntres & Obites in the Cite aforsaid [86]
the reprises nott deducted Lxix £. ~~xxiis.~~ xiiis. viiid. ob. e:
wherof Reprises yerely vii £. ~~viis.~~ viiis. id. e: p:
And so Remayns Clere Lxii £.^ vs. viid. ob. [^] ~~xvs. vid. ob~~. p:

[f.15v] Hundred de Radlowe

Radlow: Weston Beggard: Our Lady Chantry

[23a] The Rentall of the Landes belongyng to the Chauntery of Oure Lady within the Parysh of Weston apon Fromey [87]
In primis one messuage & Lx acres of errable land in the tenure of Rychard Walwyn Lxs.
Item a chef rent of Rychard Cromp out of the landes of Rychard lying in Bartester xiid.
Item a chef rent of Thomas Monyngton for hys landes in Weston vid.
Item a chef rent of Roger Bodnaham vid.
Item a chef rent of Rychard Tyrold id. ob. or els lb. of cummyn
Item a chef rent of Rychard Cutt id. ob.
Item a chef rent of John Bluett id. ob.
Item a chef rent of Roger Heynys iis. vid.
Item a chef rent [of] Rychard Roke id. ob. or els lb. of cummyng
Item a mese in the tenure of Thomas Gardner iiis.
Item a mese in the tenure of John Abadam viiis.
Item a mese in the tenure of Rychard Penye iiiis.

---

[83] All the chantry possesssions were sold to Hungate & Aynesworth, apart from 18s. 6d. sold to Rogers & Veale.
[84] This amount is also shown in an auditors' use grid.
[85] The 10d. has been crossed through, but the arithmetic suggests that it should not have been.
[86] Not including the cathedral. The sections included here are 7 to 22 , but the gross and net totals here are 17s. 4d. less than the actual totals of the sections, which is the amount of the error in the net total of section 7, *q.v.*
[87] The whole valuation-list has been crossed through. In this edition this footnote will take the place of the striking through so that the details can be more easily read. This includes the Reprises and the parish total set out below.

Item a mese in the tenure of Thom*as* More iiiis.
Item a ten*emen*te in the tenure of John Tumkyns xs. iiiid.
[*Total*] iiii £. xiiiis. iiiid.
M*emorandum* that the said churche ys w*ith*in the Duchie of Lancaster and charged ther [88]

[f.16] Rep*rises*
In p*ri*mis payd to the kynges ma*ies*te yerely viiid.
Item to kyng for gren*e* waxe iiiis.
Item to the kyng for [a] certen quyt rent xiid.
Item to John Lyne for [a] certayn rent xiid.
[*Total reprises*] vis. viiid.
Reman*et* clar*e* iiii £. viis. viiid.

Radlow: Stoke Edith: Our Lady Chantry

23b. Radlow Hundred The Rentall of All the Land*es* belongyng to the Chant*ery* of O*ur* Lady w*ith*in the P*ar*yshe Churche of Stoke Edythe [89]
In p*ri*mis a ten*emen*te w*ith* c*er*ten land*es* in the tenure of Thomas Savaker xxiiis. iiiid. e:
Item a ten*emen*te w*ith* a plowland in ye teno*ur* of Rog*er* Mayes vi £. e:
Item one ten*emen*te w*ith* c*er*ten land*es* in the tenure of Robart Hoggys & John ap Thomas viiis. e:
Item a ten*emen*t w*ith* a garden in the tenure of Rob*er*t Hogges iis. e:
Tot*alis* isti*us* cant*arie* vend*itur* Johan*ni* Hereff*ord* & Ric*ardo* Willys*on*
[*Total*] vii £. xiiis. iiiid. p:
wherof: Rep*rises*
In p*ri*mis payd to John ap Thomas for c*er*ten land*es* ther a red rose
Item p*aid* oute of the land*es* & ten*emen*tes called Brownes iiis. xid. e:
Item payd to M*aste*r Lyngen xiid. e:
Item p*aid* to the Shreve of the Shere [90] xiid. e:
Item to be dystrubyted to ye poore people in the p*ar*yshe of Stoke vis. viiid. e:
Item to John Lyngh*am* esquyer going out of the land*es* in the tenur of Savaker go p*er* ann*um* ixs. [91] e:
[*Total reprises*] xxis. viid. p:
exon*er*and*um*
Reman*et* clare vi £. xis. ixd. e:

Radlow: Ledbury: Trinity Service

24. Radlowe Hundred The S*er*vys of the Trynyte in Ledburye
In p*ri*mis a ten*emen*te in ye tenure of ye incu*m*bent*es* ixs. e:
Item a ten*emen*te in the tenure of John Chamber iiiis. e:
Item a ten*emen*t in the tenure of John Hyll iis. iiiid.
Item a ten*emen*te in the tenure of James Mayle viiis. e:
[f.16v] Item a ten*emen*te in the tenure of Edward Hewys iiiis. vid. e:
Item a ten*emen*te in the tenure of Annes Marlyon iiiis. vid. e:
Item a ten*emen*te in the tenure of the Incu*m*bent*es* iiiis.
Item a ten*emen*te in the tenure of John Benys xiiis. iiiid. e:
Item a ten*emen*te in the tenure of John Laryman viis. vid. e:
Item a ten*emen*te in the tenure of Rychard Fermor viis. e:
Item a ten*emen*te in the tenure of John Wattes viis. vid. e:
Item a ten*emen*te in the tenure of Elzabeth Zyblyz iiiis. e:
Item a ten*emen*te in the tenure of John Hyll iis. vid.
It*em* a ten*emen*te in the tenure of John Skynn*er* xiid. e:
Item a ten*emen*te in the tenure of the Incumbent*es* iis. vid.
Item a ten*emen*te in the tenure of Rychard Nashe iis. e:

---

[88] Properties within the Duchy of Lancaster were valued separately; see section 29.
[89] See section 6d.; 20s. income of the obits of Roger Hore and John Pratte charged here.
[90] 'to the sheriff of the shire (county)'
[91] This line was written in a different hand from the other lines and written after them, but before the 'examinatur' annotation.

Item a ten*emen*te in the tenure of Thomas Welshman vid. e:
Item a ten*emen*te in the tenure of Gryffyth Davys viiid. e:
Item a ten*emen*te in the tenure of Hughe Donbruge iiiis. e:
Item a ten*emen*te in the tenure of Thomas Turn*er* iiiid. e:
Item a ten*emen*te in the tenure of John Gybbys w*ith* a garden nichil
Item dyv*er*s land being in dyv*er*s mens hand*es* letten by the thurdesheff p*er* ann*um* xlviis. iid. [92]

[*Total*] ~~iiii £. ixs. iid.~~ vi £. xvis. iiiid. p:

wherof: Rep*r*ises
In p*r*imis X*risto*p*h*or*o* Herefford [93] vs. ixd.
Item Thomas Clynton iiid. ob.
Item Rectori sup*er*ior*i* vid.
Item Rectori inferior*i* xvid.

[*Total reprises*] viis. xd. ob. p:
exon*eratur* p*er* Hereford & Wyllyson
Reman*et* clare vi £. viiis. vd. ob.

Radlow: Ledbury; St. Anne's Chantry

[f.17] **25**. Hundred of Radlowe The Rentall of All the Land*es* & Ten*emen*tes belo*n*gyng to the Chaunt*er*y of S. Ane in Ledbury
In p*r*imis the homehowse now in ye teno*ur* of + John Stone Liiis. ixd. e: e:
Item xl acres of errable land & old pasto*ur* + in the tenure of [^] the said [^] John Stone xiiis. iiiid.
Item on*e* medowe in the tenure of John + Stone iiiis. e:
Item a medowe in the tenure of John Holder vis. viiid.

in the N. Streete

It*em* a ten*emen*te in the tenure of the ~~seyd~~ + Incumbent vs. e: e: [94]

N*ota*tur this vis. viiid. *pro* p*ra*to is not expressed in the p*a*rtic*lars* but there is one cotage of vs. more then is here ? m*en*teyned ? lieing at Newstret yat in the t*enure* of John ? Spic*er* Therfore ?contineu the charg of vis. viiid. for the medow in the te*nure* of John Holder until further proof therof be made &c

It*em* on*e* ten*emen*te with a garden in ye tenure of John Benys viiis. e: e:
Item a shop in the tenure of John Smyth + iiis. iiiid. e: e:
Item a ten*emen*te nowe voyde + vs. e:
Item a ten*emen*te in the tenure of John Pewterer + viiis. e: e:
It*em* half a burgage in the tenure of Phylyp + Davys iiis. iiiid. e: e:

vend*itur* Joha*n*ni Hereford & Ric*ard*o Wilison

Item a ten*emen*te in the tenure of John Wyllys + vis. e: e:
It*em* on*e* par*c*ell of Barbers medow in ye tenure of Thomas + Toode iiis. iiiid. e: e:
Item on*e* myll in the tenure + of John Hyll iis. xd. e: e:
It*em* on*e* ann*u*yte of [the] Hospytall + of Ledbury xiid. e: e:
Item a garden in the tenure of Rychard Geram + iiiid. e: e:
Item a chef rent out of Gatleys land + in ye parysh of Estoner id. e: e:

[*Total*] vi £. iiiis. p:

+ n*otatu*r tot*um* cantar*ia* vend*itur* Joha*n*ni Hereford & Ric*ar*do Wileson [95]
Tot*um* vendi*tur* Jo:[*hanni*] Hereford & Ric*ardo* Wilison

Rep*r*ises
In p*r*imis to the Byshop of Herefford iiis. viid. e:
Item pa*i*d to the pa*r*sonage of ye ~~Neither~~ ^ Upper [^] Hall of Ledbury xxiid. e:
Item pa*i*d to John Lu*m*bart m*er*cha*u*nt of London xxd. e:
Item pa*i*d to the pa*r*son of the Nether Halle ther xviiid. e:
Item pa*i*d to the Bysshop of Herefford iis. viid. e:

---

[92] This item is in a different handwriting. The third sheaf of corn as rent; I am indebted to John Freeman for this suggestion.
[93] This is odd. The abbreviation for 'Christopher' is not unlike the abbreviation for 'Episcopus' which may have been the intended meaning, so: 'Ep*iscopo* Hereffordi*ensi*', that is, 'to the Bishop of Hereford'.
[94] Every item in this list, except John Holder's meadow is marked with the symbol •.
[95] This marginal note is in the middle of the longer marginal note above and was evidently written first. The '+' which seems to introduce it may relate to the properties in the list also marked '+'.

Item to the parsonage of the Over Hall for acquyt rent xviiid. e:
Item paid to Master Clynton for a chef rent iiiid. e:
Item to the mayntannaunce of a lampe iid. e:
[*Total reprises*] xiiis. iid. p:

? partum exoneratur per Jo:[*hannem*] Hereford & Ricardum Wilison

exoneratur per Jo:[hannem] Hereford & Ricardum Wilison [96]

Remanet clare Cxs. xd. p:

Radlow: Ledbury: Our Lady Chantry

[f.17v] **26**. The Rentroll of the Landes belonging to the Chauntery of Our Lady within the Parysh Churche of Ledbury

In primis one close in the tenure of William Tayler iiis. viiid. e:
Item one medowe in the tenure of Robert Bechaumpe xis. e:
Item a medowe in the tenure of Edward Benys vis. viiid. e:
Item a barn & a close in the tenure of ye Incumbent iiiis. e:
Item John Pedmore for one burgage iiis. iiiid. e:
Item William Ketherminster for one burgage iiis. iiiid. e:
Item Thomas Broke for one mese xis. e:
Item Thomas Baylye for one burgage [97] iiiis. viiid. e:
Item one rydge of land in ye tenure of the [^] sayd [^] incumbent vid. e:
Item ~~a~~ ^one [^] Smyth for one shope iis. e:
Item Gryffyth Tayler for a pece of vacant ground xiid. e:
Item John Poele for a shoppe xiid. e:
Item Rychard Taylor for a burgage iiis. e:
Item Thomas Braunche for ii burgages vs. e:
Item the seyd incumbentes howse viiis. e:
Item Rychard Taylor for a shoppe iis. e:
Item one tenemente in the tenure of Hewe Asshe viiis. e:
Item John Laryman for ii shoppes iiiis. e:
Item Henry Marche for one burgage iis. vid. e:
Item of the Hospytall xiid. e:
Item Rychard Wyllyson for one medowe vs. viiid.
Item Thomas Tood for pastures xiis. e:
Item John Skynner for ii acres of land viiid. e:
Item Elzabethe Skynner for iii acres of land viiid. e:
Item Margrett Heyward for one medo & certen landes ixs. e:
Item Thomas Mutlowe for one medow & certen landes xs. e:
Item John Hyll for one myll xvis. e:
Item Harry Clerke for one tenemente xs. e:
Item James Wynneat for iii acres of land iis. e:
Item William Elton for certen landes xxvis. viiid. e:
Item John Corryor for one burgage and a garden iis. vid. e:
Item the sayd incumbent hath xxx^ti acres at the thrudsheff [98] xxs. e: [99]
Item Edmond Baldewine for one medowe ploke iis. viiid. e:
[*Total*] ~~x £. xs. xd~~. x £. iiis. vid. p:

Totalis Cantarie Beate Marie venditur Johanni Hereford & Ricardo Willison

venditur Johanni Hereford & Ricardo Willison whereof Notatur Ther is viiid. per annum for iiii acres of lande in tenure [of] Gilbert Glover ? more charged & solde by thes particulers then is therin conteyned

[f.18] Reprises

In primis to the Bysshop of Hereford xxiiiis. e:

[96] The two notes, not quite identical, are respectively in the right and left hand margins.

[97] See section 53c.

[98] Taking the third sheaf of the corn tithes was a form of clerical income; I owe this explanation to John Freeman.

[99] This and the next line are at the top of the next page and were originally within a separate small bracket which has been struck through and then linked with the bracket which serves the total given below in this edition.

It*em* to the Ov*er*hall — iiiis. e:
It*em* to Thomas Clynton gent. — iiis. id. e:
It*em* to the fyndyng of a lampe — xiiid.

[*Total reprises*] — xxxi~~is~~. ~~iid~~.[100]

exon*eratur per* Jo:[*hannem*] Hereford & Ric*ardu*m Willason

Reman*et* clare — viii £. xiis. vd.

N*otatu*r: M*emorandum* ther was pr*e*sented befor the comyssion*er*s one shop in the tenur of Hewgh Woodward at iis. viiid. by yere and vi acres of land in the ten*ure* of Peter Lawraunce at iiiis. viiid. by yere which som*m*es was never paidd and above nott charged in the totall som*me*.

Radlow: Bosbury

27. The Rentrol[l++] of the Land*es* belo*n*gyng to the P*ar*yshe Church of Bosburye
In p*ri*mis John Hope for a ten*emen*te — vis. viiid.
It*em* of Thomas Farley for a c*er*ten land — iiiis. xd.
It*em* of Morice Dodyng for a mene w*ith* a close — iiiis.
It*em* of John Alcote for ii acr*es* of errable land — viiid.
It*em* of Rouland Bocher for a cotage — iis.
~~It*em* for a p*ar*cell of land nowe voyde — n*ichi*l~~
It*em* Rychard Blackwey for a medowe — vis. viiid.
It*em* Wyllyam Wodhyn for a cotage — vis. viiid.
It*em* of hym for a other cotage — iiiis. viiid.
It*em* of Humfre Powell for a cotage — vis. viiid.
It*em* of John Knyght for a close — xis.
It*em* of Rychard Nasshe for a rent goyng out of hys frehold — xiiid. ob.
It*em* of John Harford gent. for one acre of past*ur* — viiid.
It*em* of the same John for iii acres of errable la*n*d — xviiid.
It*em* of Rych*ard* Bakon for on*e* acre of errable land — vd.
[18v] It*em* of John Worre for a yerely rent of the frehold of Thomas Kent — iiid.
It*em* of Rychard Broye for a chef rent — iid.
It*em* of Rychard ap Powell for a rent — iid.
It*em* a yerely rent out of the land*es* of John Taylor — id.
It*em* of James Bryge for a rent out of hys land*es* — id.
It*em* a yerly rent out of ye land*es* of Rychard Wodyng — id.

[*Total*] — Lviiis. iiiid. ob. p:[101]

Rep*ri*ses
In p*ri*mis payd yerely to the Byshop of Her*eford* — viiis.
It*em* to John Chambyrlayn for a chef rent — viid.

[*Total reprises*] — viiis. viid.

And so remayn*s* clere — xlixs. ixd. ob.

Radlow: Bishops Frome; Our Lady Chantry

28. The Rentroll of the Landes belongyng to ye S*er*vyce of O*ur* Lady w*ith*in the P*ar*yshe Church of Byshop Frome
In p*ri*mis of Rouland Boyse for a ten*emen*te with thapp*er*ten*au*nces — xxviiis. viiid.
It*em* of Mauld*e* Boyse wedowe on*e* ten*emen*te — xxiiiis.
It*em* of Rychard Benet for on*e* ten*emen*te — xs.
It*em* of Rychard Hunt for on*e* closse — xxd.
It*em* of John Wyer for ii acres & d*imidietat*i of errable land — xid.

vend*itur* Reve & Johnson

It*em* of Katern*e* Fyssors that she payeth for the foxe — iis.
It*em* of Rychard Benett for c*er*ten land — ~~xiiiis.~~

canc*ellatu*r quom*inus*q*ue* melius examinat*ur*[102]

[*Total*] ~~iiii £. xvd.~~ — Lxviis. iiid. p:

---

[100] The total of 32s. 2d. has been amended to read 31s. 1d.
[101] This total appears on the previous page against a bracket linking all the items above.
[102] It is cancelled so that it may be better examined. See section 53c.

wherof: Rep*ri*ses

In p*ri*mis payd oute of Roland Boysse land	iis.
Item paid out of Rychard Benett*es* ten*emen*te to the Bysshop of Heref*ord*	viiis.
It*em* of ye ii acr*es* that John Wyer holdyth to ye canon*s* backhowse	iiid.

exoner*atur per* Reve et Johnson

[*Total reprises*]	~~xis. iiid.~~	xs. iiid. p:
Reman*et* clare	~~Lxxis.~~	Lviis. p:

Radlow: Bishops Frome: Lamplight

[28a] A Lamplyght

Item that there is one acre of land in the tenure of Katheryne Fytzusse gyven to her mayntenaunce of a lamplyght in the said paryshe yerly — viiid. e:

Radlow: Lugwardine: Chantry of the Trinity, St. Anne and All Saints

[f.19] **[28b]** [103] Hundred de Radlowe: Lugwardyn, Decanat*us* de Weston

The Certyficatt of David Richard*es* Clerk Vicare of the P*ar*ishe Churche of Lugwardyn and John Treharen and Wil*lia*m Warg*ea*unt t[*he] Churche wardynes there and Edmund Skyr[*m] and Myles Chamb[er]lyne p*ar*ysh*io*ners there

In p*ri*mis they sey that w*i*thin the seid p*ar*ishe churche there is a chauntrie callid Will*ia*m Stourtons cha*u*nt[ry] founded by the seid Will*ia*m Stourton in the honor of the Blessed ~~Lady~~ Trynyte, O*ur* Lady Seynt Anne and All Seyntes And that one Will*ia*m Hyggyn*s* clerk a man of verie honest behavyor and competently learnyd ys nowe ^ precher [^] incombent of the seyd chauntrie and that certeyn custom*ary* land*es* and ten*ementes* of the yerely value of Cvis. viiid. holden of John War*m*combe esquier as of his manor of Lugwardyne by the yerely rent of xxvs. xid. ob. and other s*er*veces accordyng to the custome of the seyd mannor were belonging unto the seyd chauntrie w*i*th land*es* and tenement*es* the seyd Wil*lia*m Hygge*n*s at his furst comyng unto the sayd chauntrie toke to holde by copye of courte rolle of Ric*ard* Warncombe then lord of the seyd manor and payd therfore to ? fyne viii £. as by court rolle therof made redy to be showed more playnely ~~maye~~ ^ mighte [^] appere and that in lyke manner the p*re*dycessors of the sayd Will*ia*m Hyggyns at there fyrst comyng to the sayd chauntrye toke the seyd land*es* and tenement*es* of the lord*es* of the sayd mannor as by certen other court rolles redy allso to be showed more playnely ~~maye~~ myte appere the certenty of whiche land*es* and tene*mentes* apperyth in a cedule hereunto annyxed and further they saye that there is no other land*es* tenement*es* or heredytament*es* belonging to the seyd chauntrye but only the sayd custom*ary* landes & ten*emen*tes in the said cedule specefyed

[f.19v] Item they saye that there is no chalys or ornament unto the said chauntre belongyng

Item they saye there is not w*i*thin the sayd p*ar*ishe any college, frechapell or stypendary pr*ie*st

Item they saye there is not any land*es* tene*mentes* or other heredytament*es* gevyn to the fynding of any ~~shole~~ sole pr*ie*st lamp light obyt or annyv*er*sarie w*i*thin the seid p*ar*ishe churche

Item there is w*i*thin the seid p*ar*ishe and a hundred of howselyng people

Item that the vicarege of the seyd parishe churche is worth by yere — x £.

Ex*aminatur per* Wil*lelmum* Crowche [104]

---

[103] The numbering in the original document is awry. Both Bishops Frome and Lugwardine are given the number '28'. In order to preserve for referencing purposes as much of the original numbering as possible, it has seemed best to use the suffixes 'a', 'b' and 'c'.

[104] The statements given above have the appearance of formal answers to a standard set of interrogatories.

28c [105] [f.20] The Chauntre of the Trynite, Our Lady and Sent Anne & Alsayntes in the Parishe ^ Churche [^] of Lugwarden

The Copie of ye Rentall of the Custom*ary* Land*es* belongyng to the Chauntre

In primis one mease and Lx acres of custumary landes called Wetheres, one rugge of land conteynyng half an acre and the thyrde p*ar*tie of an acre of pasture called Wethers more

It*em* one mese called Capiesplace

It*em* one crofte conteynyng in hitself ii acres of land custumary and one other mease called Hall Croft conteyn*ing* in hit self iiii acres of land custumar*y*

It*em* one mease and one crofte called Tullyngtons conteynyng in hit self one acre and a half of custum*ary* [land] and one other mease w*ith* a croft being late Will*ia*m Elyes conteynyng in hit self ii acres & a half [^] of [^] custumari land and thre acres of medowe grownd lying in Kyng*es* Hey w*ith* thapp*er*ten*aun*ces in Lugwarden of sokeland

It*em* one crofte theyre conteynyng in hit self one acre of custum*ary* land of sokeland called Cock*es* Close and one mese contaynyng in hit self one acre of land custum*ary* of sokland there called the Scholemasters Place

[f. 20v] It*em* iii acres of land custumary there in sokeland late of Thomas Hulles and viii acres of land custum*ary* of sokeland whych was lat*e* Will*ia*m Ellys land

It*em* one mease there conteynyng in hit self one acre of custum*ary* land called Le Fyshers and one mease conteynyng in hit self one acre of land custum*ary* called Bellamyes

It*em* one mease there ~~called~~ conteynyng in hit self one acre of custum*ary* land late Will*ia*m Baylyes

It*em* one mease there called Pretewood*es* conteynyng in hit self one acre of land custum*ary* and one mease there called Redes conteynyng iiii acres of land custum*ary*

It*em* xix acres and a half of custum*ary* land and iii acres of medowe grownde in Kyngeshey of sokeland and one mease there called Reese Closes cont*eynyng* in hit selff the moytie of one acre of land custum*ary* of sokeland

It*em* one mese there conteynyng in hit self one acre and a half acre custum*ary* land of sokelond called Hamons Close and one medowe called Monsall cont*eynyng* by estimat*io*n iiii acres of custum*ary* landes

[f.21] It*em* ii acres and a half of medowe of custum*ary* land lying in Kyngeshey

All whiche p*re*mysses hath ben and remayned contynually by the space of xx yeres and more in the manuraunce and occupation of the chauntre pryst*es* and ar valued by estymat*io*n at the yerely rent of — Cvis. viiid.

wherof in

In rent resolute going oute of the p*re*misses to the Mayer & Baylyes of the Citie of Herefford for a medowe called Monshall — xiid.

Also the rent resolute paid to John Warnecombe esquyer chefe lord there for the said copiehold land*es* by yere — xxvs. xid. ob.

Also the rent resolut*e* paid to the Deane and Chapiter of the Cathedrall Church of Heref*ord* going out of the p*re*myssez by yere — iid.

S*u*m of rent*es* resolut*es* — xxviis. id. ob.

And so remayneth clere — Lxxixs. vid. ob.

Ex*aminatu*r p*er* Will*elmu*m Sayer deput*atem* Will*el*mi Crowch sup*er*vis*or*is

[f. 21v] The hole some of the all the within wrytten acres amounteth to Cxxv acres ^ and a halfe & athe threde parte of an acre [^] of custumary lande

[105] See the previous footnote but one.

[f. 22r & v.][*blank*]

Radlow: Yarkhill

[f.23] **29** The Rentall of All the Landes & Stokes belongyng to the mentenaunce of Lyghtes & Lampes in ye Parysh of Yarkyll

In p*ri*mis John Tomkyns holdyth iii acr*es* of land*es* viiid.

It*em* Roger Palmer holdyth one acre vid.

It*em* Walt*er* Dyer kypyth one cowe p*ri*ce xiiis. iiiid. the rent iis.

[*Total*] ~~iiis. iid~~.

w*ith*in the Duche of Lancaster charged [106]

Radlow: Lugwardine: Our Lady & St. Anne's Chantry

[f.23] **30.** [107] The Content*es* of the Customary Land*es* belongy*ng* to the Chaunt*ery* of O*u*r Lady & S. Annes in the P*ar*yshe Church of Luggewardyne

In p*ri*mis on*e* mese and Lx acres of customery land*es* & on*e* rudge of land co*n*teynyng di*midie* acre & thurde p*ar*te of a acre of past*ur* called Wetheres more

It*em* on*e* mese called Copye Place

It*em* on*e* croft ii acres of land custumery and on mese called Hawe Croft conteyn*ing* in hyt self iiii acres of land

It*em* on*e* mese and on*e* crofte called Tyllyngtons conteynyng in hyt self on*e* acre and di*midie* of customery [land] and one other mese w*ith* a croft beyng lately Will*iam* Elyzes co*n*teynyng in hyt self ii acres & a half of customery land iii acres of medow ground lying in Kyng*es* Hey w*ith* thapp*er*ten*aun*ces in Lugwardyn of sokeland

It*em* one croft there conteynyng in hyt self on*e* acre of customery land of sookland called Cock*e* Closse and one mese contaynyng in hyt self on*e* acre of land customery of sokeland ther called the Skolmasters Place

It*em* iii acres of custumary land ther in sokelond late of Thomas Hules & viii acres of land custom*ery* of sokeland wh*i*ch was Will*iam* Elyes land

It*em* on*e* mese ther conteynyng in hyt self on*e* acr*e* of custom*ery* land called Leye Fysshers & on*e* mese conteynyng in hyt self on*e* acr*e* of custom*ery* land called Bellemes

[f. 23v] It*em* on*e* mese ther conteynyng in hyt self on*e* acre of custom*ery* land late Will*iam* Baylys

It*em* on*e* mese ther called Pretiewood*es* conteynyng in hyt self on*e* acre of land custom*ery* & one mese ther called Redes conteynyng iiii acres of land customery

It*em* x acres di*midie* of custom*ery* land and iiii acres of medo ground in Kyngeshey of sokeland and on*e* mese ther called Res Close conteynyng in hyt selff the moyete of on*e* acre of [land] custom*ery* of sokeland [108]

It*em* on*e* mese ther conteynyng in hyt self on*e* acre di*midie* custom*ery* land of sokelond called Hamonscloce and on*e* medowe called Monssell cont*eynyng* by estimat*i*on iiii acres of custom*ery* land

It*em* ii acres and a half of medowe of customery land lying in Kyngeshey

All whiche p*re*mysses hath ben and remayneth contynually by the space of xx yeres and more in the memorance and occupat*i*on of the seyd chaunt*ery* p*ri*est*es* and ar valued at the yerely [rent] of v £. vis. viiid. Cvis. viiid. e:

wherof: Rep*ri*ses

In p*ri*mis payd to the kyng*es* bayly of Heref*ord* for a medowe called Monshall xiid.

---

[106] Charged within the separate valuations of the duchy and therefore deleted here.

[107] Section 3 is another version of section 28c.

[108] This item bears little resemblance to the earlier version at 28c above. But the total at the end is unchanged.

It*em* John Warnecombe esquyer chefe lord ther for the sayd
coppye land*es* xxvs. xid. ob.
Item to the Deane and Chapytur of the Cath*edral* Church of Herefford iid. e:
[*Total reprises*] xxviis. id. ob. p :
S*um*m*a* clar*e* Lxxixs. vid. ob.

Radlow Totals

[30a] Totalis xlii £. xs. id. ob. p:
S*um*m of the hole ch*aun*t*r*es in the Hundred of Radlowe
xlii £. ~~iiis. id. ob~~. ~~xiiid. ob~~. xs. id. ob. p:
wherof Rep*r*ises yerely Cxixs. ~~ixd~~. viiid. p: e:
And so rem*ains* xxxvi £. ~~iiiis. iiiid~~. ~~xvid. ob~~. xvs. vd. ob. [109]

Broxash: Much Cowarne: Our Lady Service

[f. 24] Hundred de Broxas:
31 The Land*es* that belongyth to the Sarves of O*ur* Lady w*ith*in the Church of Muche Cowarne
In p*ri*mis ii mesuages & one yard land in the teno*ur* of John Mason the rent xxvis. viiid. e:
It*em* a mesuage & vii acres of land in the tenure of Walt*er* Jauncye vis. viiid. e:
It*em* one cotage in the tenure of Thomas Saubery iiis. iiiid. e:
It*em* for c*er*ten landes in the tenure of John Boudge called Squyers viiis. iiiid. e:
Item a rent goyng owte of the land*es* of Thom*as* Butler iis. e:
Sum*ma* xlviis. p:
vend*untur* Ranulpho Burgh & Rob*er*to Beverley
Exit*us* fest*o* Pasch*alis* anno ii°
vend*untur* ut sup*ra* wherof
Reddit*us* resolut*us*
In p*ri*mis payd to Rychard Paunsett esquyer owte of the land called Squyers vs.
exoner*atur* p*er* p*re*fatos Ranulphu*m* & Rob*er*tu*m*
Sum*ma* vs. e:
Et reman*et* clar*e* xliis. e.

Broxash: Much Cowarne: Lamp

[31a] Lamp Land
Item a c*er*ten close lying in Cowarn*e* in the tenure of John Seward towardes the menten*a*unce of a lampe & ys called Lamp Closse xid. e:

Broxash: Marden: Chantry

32 The Land*es* y*a*t belong to the Chaunt*ery* of M*ar*den
In p*ri*mis Thom*as* Taylor holdyth a ten*emen*t w*ith* thapp*er*ten*a*unces xxvis. viiid.
Item Walter Dyar holdyth ii ten*emen*tes w*ith* ye app*er*ten*a*unces viiis.
Item Hew Ext*on* holdyth on*e* ten*emen*t w*ith* ye app*er*ten*a*unces xis. iiiid.
Item Hewe Love holdyth ii ten*emen*tes w*ith* the app*er*ten*a*unces viiis.
Thomas Cooke holdyth on*e* ten*emen*te iis. iiiid.
Item Thom*as* Baker holdyth c*er*ten land*es* vs. iiiid.
It*em* Ric*hard* Shep*p*ard hold on*e* ten*emen*te w*ith* thapp*er*ten*a*unces iiiis.
[f.24v] Item Syr Harry Stevyns holdyth a ten*emen*te w*ith* thapp*er*ten*a*unces xxxiiis. iiiid.
Sum*ma* iiii £. xixs. p:
vend*untur* Rog*er*o Hereford & Joh*an*ni P*re*diaux
wherof

[109] Each of the struck through sets of figures was in its turn marked 'probatur' or 'examinatur'.

Rep*ri*ses Chef Rent
In p*ri*mis the sayd Harry Stevyns payth out of the seyd howse to the Quene [110] ~~xiiis~~.
can*cellatur* extinguit*ur*
The same Harry Stevyns payth to John Harper xd. e:
The sayd Harry Stevyns pay*e*th to John Lyngen esquyer for the same howse vid. e:
The same Harry pay*e*th oute of the same house to the Deane & Chapytur of Herefford vd. e:
[*Total reprises*] ~~xiiiis. ixd~~. xxid. p:
Tot*um* exone*ratur* *per* Rog*erum* Hereford & Joh*ann*em P*re*diaux
S*umma* rep*ri*ses
S*umma* clare iiii £. ~~vs~~. iiiis. iiid. [111] p:

Broxash: Marden: Trinity Service

33. The Land*es* belongyng to the Stypendary P*ri*est of the Trynyte S*e*rvys in M*ar*den
In p*ri*mis John Byrry holdyth on*e* ten*emen*te w*ith* the app*er*ten*a*unces xs. iid. e:
vend*itur* Rog*er*o Hereford & Joh*ann*i P*re*diaux
wherof: Rep*ri*ses
It*em* John Berry pay*e*th yerely out of the seyd ten*emen*t for a chef rent ~~xviiid.~~
extinguit*ur*
It*em* the same John Berry payth yerely oute of the sayd tenement to John Lyngen squyer viiid. e:
exone*ratur* *per* eosdem Hereford & P*re*diaux
S*umma* rep*ri*ses iis. iid. p: [112]
S*umma* clar*e* viiis. e:

Broxash: Marden: Lamps and Lights

[f. 25] **34** The Re[n]ttall of the Land*es* & Mony to the Fyndyng of Lamp*es* & Lyght*es* in M*ar*den
In p*ri*mis Thomas Wotton clarke holdyth on*e* acre of errable land called Lampe Acre vid.
It*em* John Tayl*ou*r of Wellyngton payeth to the fyndyng of the sayd lyght*es* oute of the land*es* of the cha*un*ter*y* of Wellyngton iiiid.
S*umma* xd. p:

Broxash: Sutton St. Nicholas: Chantry

35 The Land*es* belongyng to the Chaunt*ery* of S. Nycolas in Sutton
In p*ri*mis on*e* mese & xxi acres of errable land & ii acres of medo in the tenure of John Spens*er* xxxiiis. iiiid. e:
vend*itur* Reve & Johnson
?sus*pensus* reddit*us* xxiiis. iiiid. debet
et sic exone*ratur*
It*em* oute of the medowe of Thomas Seborn called Myll Medowe vis. viiid.
S*umma* xls.

M*emorandum* that for asmoche as the mes*e* & land*es* aboveseid in the tenure of John Spenc*er* is charged with xs. by yere more then ev*er* was p*aid* as it appereth in the examination therof therfor it is nowe judged that the baily shal not be charged but after xxiiis. iiiid. p*er* Joh*ann*em Jauncey

[110] Queen Catherine Parr. She married Edward Seymour, duke of Somerset, in June 1547, but would have continued to have been entitled to these revenues. She died on 7 Sep. 1548.
[111] An auditors' use grid in the margin gives this figure, which is before the 13s. was struck through..
[112] The total before 18d. was struck out.

Broxash: Bodenham: Our Lady Service

36 The Land*es* belongyng to Our Lady Serves in Bodna*m*
In p*ri*mis Will*ia*m Rece holdyth one mese with c*er*ten land*es* Lis. iid.
It*em* a cotage in the tenure of Alys Mason iiiis. viiid.
It*em* Rog*er* Edward*es* holdyth c*er*ten land*es* in Bodna*m* xxiis. xd.
It*em* Rychard ap Yevan holdyth a close in Bodna*m* iis. iiiid.
It*em* John Morice holdyth a close in Bodnam iiiis. id. e:

cu*m particulis*
vend*itur* no*min*e cotag*ii* et uni*us* [+++] [113]
W:*illelmo* Fountayne et Ric*ardo* Mayne

It*em* oute of the land*es* of Walt*er* Hare cald Bowleys Medowe iiiid.
It*em* John Went on*e* close in the more xvid. e:

cu*m particulis*
vend*itur* eisdem W:*illelmo* Fowntayne & Ric*ardo* Mayne

It*em* oute of one ten*emen*te in the Cytye of Here*ford* in the
tenure of Alys Alawton wydowe iiiis.

vend*itur* Jacobo Rogers & Veale

~~Item the lord ferys~~

S*umma* iiii £. xs. ixd. p:

wherof: Rep*r*ises
In p*ri*mis Will*ia*m Rece pay*e*th out of hys mesuage to the Lord Ferrys vis.
It*em* the same Wyllyam pay*e*th oute of the seyd mese to Will*ia*m
Lucye esquyer iiis. vd.
[f.25v] It*em* the same Will*ia*m payth oute of the same mese to John Lyngen
esquyer iiid.
It*em* the same Will*ia*m [payeth] out of the seyd messe to Hugh
Welshe xviiid.
It*em* Alys Mason pay*e*th out of her cotage to the Lord Ferrys [114] viiid.
It*em* Rog*er* Edward*es* pay*e*th for c*er*ten landes in Bodnam to
Will*ia*m Lucye esquyer ~~vid.~~ vd.
It*em* Rychard ap Yevant pay*e*th for a close in Bodna*m* to the
Lord Ferrys viiid.
It*em* John Mason pay*e*th for one close to the kyng*es* maiesty id.

S*umma* rep*r*ises ~~xiis. xid.~~ xiiis. p:
S*umma* clare Lxxviii~~i~~s. ~~vid.~~ ixd. p: e:

Broxash: Bodenham: the Jesus Service

37 The Land*es* belongyng to the S*er*vys of Jesus in the P*ar*ish of Bodnam
In p*ri*mis James Wyntton holdyth one mese w*ith* the app*er*ten*a*unces xxxs. xid. e:

vend*itur* Jacobo Rogers & Veale

wherof: Rep*r*ises
It*em* the same James Wy*n*tton pay*e*th out of the same mese
to Will*ia*m Lucye esquyer vs. iiiid.

exon*eratur per* Rogers & Veale

It*em* the sayd James pay*e*th to ye kyng*es* ma*ieste* out of ye seyd mese iid.

exting*uitur* in uno possess*ione* [115]

It*em* the same James payth to the kyng*es* ma*iestie* for c*er*ten land*es*
belongyng to the late P*ri*or of Brekenocke vd.

S*umma* rep*r*ises vs. xid. p:
S*umma* clare xxvs. e:

Broxash: Avenbury: Lamps

38 Avenbury Lamppes
It*em* too acres of errable land lying in the feld*es* of Anburye in
the tenure of Thomas Boyse & Thomas Barne viiid. p:

---

[113] This resembles 'gireld iur', the meaning of which is not known.
[114] Henry Grey, who held various titles, including 'Lord Ferrers of Groby. Created duke of Suffolk 11 Oct. 1551; exec. 23 Feb. 1553/4 (*Complete Peerage*).
[115] This marginal note applies to the next item too.

Broxash: Bromyard: Bastenall's School

[f.26] **39**. Land*es* & Houses belongyng to S*ir* John Bastenall in Bromyard
Item a close called O*ur* Lady Close in the tenure of John Blunt esquyer — vis. viiid.
Item Joha*n*ne Wyght wydowe holdyth a house & a barn — xxs.
Item Elzabeth Smyth holdyth a close in Lynton — iis. N
Item Harry Hunt holdyth a barn in Mylborn & anoth*er* in Bromyard — ixs. iiiid.
Item Burge Hallyngton holdyth a howse & a closse — xiiis. iiiid.
Item Thomas Blunt of Brocanton holdyth a close — iiiis.
Item Thomas Berrowe holdyth a close in Collynton — iiiid. X
Item Phylyp Hall holdyth a howse in Crokeswall — vs. iiiid.
Item John Wedn*er*ster holdyth a close & di*midie* ? bu[r]gage — xis. iiiid.
Item John Myll holdyth [an] acre of land in Wellesfyld — iiiid. N
Item Rychard ^ Hall[^] holdyth a close lying at Alowes Myle — iis. viiid.
Item James Taylo*ur* holdyth a house at the churche style — iiis. iiiid.
Item Hewe Whorwood holdyth a house next to the churche stylle — iiis. iiiid. N
Item ii acres in the tenure of John Clarke — viiid. N
Item in the tenure of John Ball [an] acre & di*midie* — ~~xviiid.~~ vid. N

S*umma* — iiii £. iiis. iid. p:

wherof: Rep*ris*es
In p*ri*mis the chef rent*es* of all the forseyd land*es* & ten*emen*t*es* ys — xiiis. iiid. e:

S*umma* declare — Lxixs. xid. e:

Broxash: Bromyard: Hugh Watham's Service

[f.26v] **40** The Houses & Land*es* to Menteyn S*ir* Hughe Wathams Serves in Bromyard
In p*ri*mis ^ John [^] Wedn*er*ster a house in Cockeswall Strete — xs. iiiid. e:
Item John Baker holdyth a ten*emen*t ther — iiiis. e:
Item Rychard Bacu*n* a ten*emen*te in Newstrete — viiis. e:
Item Thomas ap Rychard holdyth a house — vis. viiid. e:
Item Marg*er*y Smyth holdyth a ten*emen*te in New Strete — vs. e:
Item Syble Couper holdythe a house in Shurford Strete — iiis. e:
Item John Tann*er* holdeth a house in Nonwall Strete — viiis. e:

S*umma* — xlvs. p:

vend*untur* Thome Hungate & Aynesworth

Rep*ris*es
In p*ri*mis the rent dewe to the chef lord*es* of the land*es* & ten*emen*tes aforsayd — ixs. iiid. e:

exon*erantur per* eosdem

S*umma* reprises — p*ateat* e:

S*umma* declar*e* reman*et* — xxxvs. ixd. p:

Broxash: Bromyard: Lamp Lands

40a The Lampe Land*es* ther
Item on*e* acre of errable land called the Lampe Acre in the tenure of John Blewe — iiiid. e.

vend*itur* ut sup*ra*

Broxash: Stoke Lacy: Lamps

41 Stok Lacy Lampes
Item on*e* acre of errable land at the Whore Stone in the tenure of Margret Maveld — iiid. e:

Broxash: Ocle Pychard: Our Lady Chantry

42 Ocle Pychard
Item on*e* annuyte of iis. iiiid. gevyn by one John Moreley out of hys land*es* & ten*emen*t*es* to the use of the Chaunt*er*ye of O*ur* Lady in ye sayd church — iis. iiiid. e:

Broxash: Upper Sapey: Light

42a [116] Over Sapy Lyght*e*s
Item oute of the land*e*s of Rychard Wynford to menteyn a lyght — iis. e:

Broxash Totals

[**42b**] S*um*m*a* total*is* of the Chauntres & Obitt*e*s in the Hundred
of Broxas — xxii £. xiiis. iiiid. e: p:
Rep*ri*ses yerely — Lxiiis. ~~iiid~~. iiiid. e: p:
And so rem*ains* clere — xix £. xs. ~~id~~. e. p.

Grimsworth: St. Devereux: Lamp

[f.27] **43** Hundred de Grymswood: Saynt Devereux de Irchynfyld [117]
In primis ther goythe oute of the landes of John ap Davyd
to menteyn a lampe — iid. e:

Grimsworth: Bishopston: Our Lady Chantry

44 The Landes belonging to the Chauntery of Our Lady of Bysshopton
In p*ri*mis Thomas Watters John Chamberlen John Phelpott*e*s
do hold joyntly a tene*men*te wyth curtalag*e*s ther conteynyng
xlv acres of errable lande — xvis. e:
It*e*m Rychard Watkyns pay*e*th out of Dyggas Land*e*s — xiiiid. e:
It*e*m George Eccle*y* pay*e*th out of Mellyns land*e*s by yere — iiid. e:
It*e*m John House of Medelwod holdyth c*er*ten grounde called
Medelwod in Clyfford — iiis. iiiid. e:
S*um*m*a* — xxs. ixd. p:
Totu*m* vendit*ur* Joh*an*ni Hulford & Barthe*lomeo* Broksby

Grimsworth: Wellington: Our Lady Chantry

45 The Rent*e*s belong*ing* to the Chantry of O*ur* Lady in Wellyngton
In p*ri*mis of John Taylo*ur* for on*e* mese w*ith* the app*er*ten*a*unces — Liiis.
It*e*m of John Farley for Saynt Marye House — ixs.
It*em* of Thomas Cock*e*s for O*ur* Lady House — vis. viiid.
S*um*m*a* — Lxviiis. viiid. p:
~~*notatur* [+++] sunt *par*tem [+++]~~
vend*untur* Thom*e* Hungate & Aynesurth
Rep*rise*s
It*e*m to the p*re*bendary of Wellyngton — iiis. iiiid.
It*e*m to the lord*e*s of Tyllyngton — vid.
It*e*m to the p*ar*yshe church of M*ar*den — iiiid.
It*em* to M*ast*r*e*s An Ruddall — iis. vid.
It*e*m the comon fyn*e* — viiid.
It*e*m to therle of Worcet*er* [118] — iis. iiiid.
It*e*m to Mastres An Ruddall — viiid.
It*e*m to James Brydge — viiid.
It*e*m to John Lyngen — iiiid.
exon*erantur* p*er* p*er*cuisat*ores*
S*um*m*a* rep*rise*s — xis. iiiid.
exon*erantur* p*er* p*er*quis*itores*
Et reman*et* declar*e* — Lviis. iiiid.

Grimsworth: Wellington: Lamps and Lights

[f.27v] **46** Lamps & Lyghtes Ther
It*e*m on*e* acre of medo in the tenure of the vycare called Lampe
Acre — iis. ~~viiid~~. p:
It*e*m on*e* acre of errable land in the tenure of Will*ia*m Clarke
called Lampe Acre — vid.

---

[116] In the document the number is 42, presumably an error as Over Sapey is not part of Stoke Lacy.
[117] St. Devereux was not in Grimsworth hundred but in Webtree hundred.
[118] Probably Henry Somerset, who died 26 Nov. 1549, succeeded by his son William.

Summa iis. vid. p

totum venduntur Thome Hungate & Aynsworth

Grimsworth: Hampton Bishop: Chantry

47 The Land that belongs to the Chauntery of Bysshop Hampton

In primis the farmer ther iiii £. iiis. xid.

Item William Bounde xviid.

Item Thomas Lane xviiid.

Item William Cowarn xvid.

Item vii acres of wod in the parysh of Fownhope nowe ix yeres growyth

Item of Thomas Lane xd.

Summa iiii £. ixs. p:

Reprises

Item payd to the kynges maieste baylys ther viiid.

Item to the bysshop of Hereford iiid.

Item to William Herford xvid.

Item to the Cannons of Hereford xxid. ob.

Summa reprises iiiis. ob. p:

Summa declare iiii £. iiiis. xid. ob. e:

Grimsworth: Norton Canon: Stipendiary Priest

48 Norton Stipendary

In primis John Whytney doth hold one mese with iii^{xx} acres land medo & pasture xxvis. vid. [119]

Item Hewe Grey doth hold i mese with xxx acres of land medo & pasture xiis. iid. ob.

Item William Parlour holdyth i mese with a closse xxd.

Summa xls. vid. ob. p: wherof:

[f. 28] Reprises

Item owte of the tenemente in the holdyng of Whytney to the cannons of Hereford xiiis. iiiid.

Item owte of the tenemente of Hughe Greye vs. vid. ob.

Summa reprises xviiis. xd. ob. p:

Summa declare xxis. viiid. e:

Grimsworth: Mansell Lacy [120]

49 Parochia de Mansell: Lampes

Item one acre of land in the tenure of Roger Pentewall gevyn to menteyn a lampe iiiid. e:

venditur Thome Hungate & Aynesworthe

Torches: Item xviiid. by yere gevyn out of the frehold of John Amore to menteyn certen torches xviiid.

Grimsworth: Credenhill: Our Lady Service

50 Parochia de Cradnyll to the Servys of Our Lady ther

Item ii tenementes in the tenure [of] Davyd Morrys & John Taylour viiis.

venditur dictis Thome Hungate & Aynsworthe

Grimsworth: Pipe: Lamp

51 Pype Church Lampe Lande

Item i acre of land lying in Lydefyld in the tenure of Thomas Baughe iiid. p: e:

venditur eisdem Hungate & Aynsworth

[119] This could read either 6d. or 7d., but, in view of the total reprises, is probably meant for 8d.

[120] In 1547 Roger Pantoll and John More lived in Mansell Lacy. (*TNA: E. 179/117/164, f.* 4).

Grimsworth: Norton Canon: Lamp Lights

51a Norton Lampe Lyght*es* [121]
Item owt of the land*es* of John Chaunor [122] iiiid. John Mathowes iiiid.
Walter Eccle iiiid. of Raff Harryett*es* iiiid. to menteyn a lamp
Thomas Edward*es* iiiid. & Will*ia*m Gynond iiiid. iis.
vend*itur* in infr*adic*tis Hungate & Aynsworthe

Grimsworth: Burghill

52 Burhyll Lampe
It*em* on*e* acre of land called Lamp*e* Acre in the tenure of
Thom*as* Bennett iiiid. e:
vend*itur* eisd*em*

Grimsworth: Canon Pyon

53 Pewne Canon
It*em* on*e* acre of errable land in the teno*u*r of Rychard Bryan
to menten a p*ri*este iiiid. e:
vend*itur* ut sup*ra*

Grimsworth: Yazor

[53a] Yasar Lyght*es*
It*em* the rent of ii kyne of the bequest of Phylypp Hogg*es* to
the menten*a*uncez of torches w*i*ch kyne be in the kepyng
of Will*ia*m Hoggys xxd. e:

Grimsworth: Burghill: Tullington Chantry

[f.28v] **[53b]** The Ch*a*untre of Tullyngton in the Parishe Church*e* of Burghill
It*em* James Hill farm*er* of all the land*es* lying & being in the
same p*ar*ishe by yer xxxs. iiiid. e:
vend*itur* Joh*an*ni Perient mi*li*ti & Thome Reve

Grimsworth Totals

[53c] S*um*m totall of all the ch*a*unt*r*es & obitt*es* in the hundred of ~~Wo~~
Grymswood the ?truth deducted p: e: xiii £. ~~xiiid ob~~. ixs. iiiid. ob.
Reprises yerely p: e: xxxiiiis. iiid.
And so rem*ains* p: xi £. ~~vis. xd. ob~~. xvs. id. ob. [123]

Ex*aminatu*r p*er* Will*elmu*m Sayer, deput*atem* Will*elm*i
Crowch*e*, Sup*er*vis*oris* *Dom*ini R*e*g*is* ib*id*em

[f.29] **[53d]** M*emorandum* that here after insuy*et*h certen reformations of p*re*sentement*e*s of dyv*er*s chaunt*er*ey p*ri*estes w*ith*in the office of John Jaunceye the whyche reformatyons hathe not be only taken be supplycaton of thos that hather susteyned the wronge but also upon the examynaton of the matter by auncyon [124] men of the countrey wher the same do lye as severally hereaft*er* shall appere. [125]

In p*ri*mis wher that yt was p*re*sented by the Dene & Chapyt*er* that on*e* Kat*er*yn Hyll of Wolhope should pay yerely to the menten*a*unce of a certen obyt oute of her freehold iiis. iiiid. the truth ys that as she hath provyd by her self & also by dyv*er*s of her auncyant neyghbo*u*rs the sayd De*a*ne & Chapyter hath not be answer*e*d of no more but o^n[^]ly iiiid. by thys space of thys xl yerez wher upon the seyd iiis. ~~iiiid~~. ys remyttyd unto such tyme that better matter can be p*ro*vyd for the kynge. [126]

---

121 If this is Norton Canon, it is out of its order. Edwards and Chabnor lived in Norton Canon.
122 Prob. Chabnor.
123 The actual total is £11 12s. 1½d.
124 prob. 'ancient'.
125 The whole paragraph has been stuck through. but is left here unstruck through in the interests of legibility.
126 Also crossed through in the original. See section 6zd.

Item a certen pensyon going owte of Mascalles landes ^ late belongyng to Our Lady Chauntery in the parysh of S. Nicolas [^] admountyng to the yerely valure of ixs. ys dyscharged for that the collector therof can not enquiere wher any such landes do lye & also any such pencyon hath not be payd by the space of the remembraunce of any man in the parysh nowe beyng a lyve. [127]

[f. 29v] Memorandum that ^ ther [^] were ii parcelles more presented in ~~thys~~ the chauntery of Ledbury called [^] Our Lady Chauntry [^] one parcell admountyng to the yerely value of iiiis. viiid. out of hys frehold & one other summ admountyng to the value of iis. viiid. goyng out of a burgage in Ledbury the whych severall summes hath not be payd by the space of thys xx yeres wherfore they be not charged in the totall summe of the sayd chaunterye. [128]

Memorandum that this some of xiiiis. by yere being in the handes of Rychard Benett is ~~nott~~ charged in the totall some of this serves ^ of Our Lady in Bysshopfrome [^] for that ytt apperythe in the presentment that one John Pychard thelder gent. margaged the landes oute of the whiche the seyed yerely rente doth issue unto the proctours of the ~~seyd~~ serves of Our Lady in Frome foresayed unto ~~whiche~~ suche tyme the same John Pychard his heyres or assignes shuld content & paye unto the seyed proctours or theyre successours the some of fyve markes & the whiche some John Pychard the yonger gent. hathe well & truely contented & payed to the handes of the accomptaunte whyche accomptaunte is redy to make payment therof to the kynges maiesties use &c. [129]

John Jauncey's Totals

[f. 30] **[53e]** Summa totalis ballivati Johannis ^ Jauncye [^] ~~Jacke~~
prima facie CC~~x~~xxiii £. viid. e: p:
Ccxxiii £. viid. p: e:
Resolutiones eiusdem ballivati inferiori proximi xxiii £. ~~xiiis.~~ iiis. viid. ob. e: p:
xxiii £. iiiis. viid. ob. p: e:
Et remanet Ciiii^{xx} xix £. ~~vis. xs.~~ xvs. xid. ob. e:
Ciiii^{xx} xix £. xvs. xid. ob. e: p: [130]

Radlow: Stoke Edith: Spicer's Anniversary

[f.30v] **[53f]** De firma unius mesuagii certis terris pratis & pasturis eidem mesuagii spectantis iacentis in Stoke Edithe vocati Spicers Place & dati per dictum Spicer ad mauntenenentem unius anniversarii in ecclesia de Stoke predicto imperpetuum nunc in tenura Johannis Frire per indenturam [131] vis. viiid.
venditur Reve & Johnson

Radlow: Park: St. James's Chapel

[53g] De firma decimarum[132] grani & feni ac aliarum decimarum ? spectantium libere capelle vocate Seynt James Chapell infr a mannorum de Parke nunc in tenura Johannis Powis infra parochiam de Ledbury xs.
exoneratur; venditur Reve & Johnson
per Johannem Jauncey deputatem supervisorem ibidem

[ff.31-32v all blank]

---

[127] This paragraph is also struck through in the original. Parish of St. Nicholas, Hereford. See section 15.

[128] This paragraph also struck through. See section 26 where the valuation of 4s. 8d. can be found, but there is no burgage (only a meadow) valued at 2s. 8d..

[129] As is this one. See section 28.

[130] Although the totals recorded above come to £200 0s. 11½d., it is clear that this is intended to be the total of the valuations of the cathedral, the Hereford city churches and the hundreds of Radlow, Broxash and Grimsworth., that is, John Jauncey's bailiwick. It leaves open where the valuations in sections 53d and 53e are accounted for.

[131] This does not appear next to the Stoke Edith chantry (section 23b), but is something of an afterthought.

[132] Farm of the tithes; 'decimarum' is represented in the text by 'X^{arumr}'

[f. 33] **[54]** The Collectyon of John Scudamor ~~of the~~ being collector of the Hundredes of Greytre Wormelow & Webtre

[ff. 33v-34v all blank]

[f. 35] The Hundred of Greytree

Greytree: Ross: Our Lady Chantry

54a [133] The Chaunt*ery* of O*ur* Lady w*ith*in the p*ary*she of Rosse

Item John Scudamor esquyer & Hewe Underwood for a mesu*age* lying in Lyttle Calowe xxvis.

vend*itur* Jacobo Rogers & Ric*ardo* Veale

Item Izott Tom*m*as for a ten*emen*t in Rosse with a garden & other land*es* ther xliiis. iiiid. e:

ten*ementum* xxiiiis. vend*itur* ut ?in p*er*quis*itione* & ~~xixs. resid'~~ xixs. iiiid. resid*uum* vend*itur* Silvestr*o* Leighe & Le[+++] ? Vayle

no*tatu*r it apperithe by the p*ar*ticlers of Tho:[*mas*] Marshe & Will*ia*ms this ?ten*emen*t be in the tenure of W:[*illiam*] Thomas charge at the valowe of xxiiiis. not as yet discharged

Item John Mutlowe for a ten*emen*t & a garden xiiis. vid.

vendit*ur* Butler &c

Item Edmond Taylo*ur* for a ten*emen*t & a garden vis. vid.

ut sup*ra*

•Item Ellyzabeth Aggas wedowe for a barn & a garden & other land*es* xs. xid.

vendit*ur* ut sup*ra*

n*otatu*r W. Hagger in l*itt*eris pat*entibus*

•Item Thomas Hall for a garden xiiiid.

vendit*ur* ut sup*ra*

in p*aten*t*ibus* l*itt*eris p*ro*ut G. Hall

Item one voyde ten*emen*te in Rosse vs.

Item a nother voyd ten*emen*t in Rosse iis. iid.

Item John Harteley for a ten*emen*te vs.

~~vend*itur* prefat*is* Rogers & Veale~~

vend*itur* Butler

~~?remanet in manu [+++]~~

Item John Belt for a garden xiid. +

vend*itur* ut sup*ra*

Item Robart Barbo*r* for a ten*emen*t & a garden w*it*h c*er*ten land*es* iiis. id. ob.

vend*itur* ut sup*ra*+

in p*ar*ticu*lis* nisi iiis. vid.

Item Rychard Nycolas for a garden iiiid.

vend*itur* ut sup*ra* +

•Item Ales a Gw*i*ll*a*m for a tenement iiis. viiid. ob.

•Item Rychard Hoell*es* for a ten*emen*te & a garden iiis. iiiid. e:

vend*itur* ut sup*ra*

Item one voyde tenemente by yere iiiis.

vend*itur* Butler +

•Item John Markye for ii ten*emen*tes & a barn garden & land*es* xxis. e:

ut sup*ra*

Item off Will*ia*m Thynne for c*er*ten land*es* in Wylton iis. iiiid. ob. e:

vend*itur* Rogers & Veale

Item off John Dewe for one dole of land iiiid.

vend*itur* Butler +

Item off Kateryng Taylo*ur* wedowe for on*e* acre vid.

vend*itur* ut sup*ra* +

Item Wyllyam Benett iii acres xiid.

vend*itur* ut sup*ra*+

Item one annuytie oute of a ten*emen*t that on*e* John Thornycroft doth dwellyng in Rosse [134] ~~vis. vid.~~

cancell*atur* quo*m*inusq*ue* melius ex*aminatu*r

[133] This is numbered '54a' in the original.

[134] See section 90b.

Item of Thomas Somner for one acre of arrable land in Clyffild
in the lordship of Walton[135] iis. iiiid.

Summa vii £. xviis. viiid. ob.

Totalis venditur Butler &c xxxvis. iiid. ob.

[f.35v] Reprises

Item Izott Thomes for a rent of a garden & a tenement to the
parson ther for chef rent iis. id.

Item Izott Tomes payth for land lying in Wylton to the Lord Grey iis.

exoneratur per Leighe & Vale [136]

Item John Mutlowe payth for a tenement in Rosse to the Bysshop
of Hereford + vid.

exoneratur per Butler &c

Item Edmond Taylour payth for a tenement in Rosse to the
Bysshope of Hereford + vid.

exoneratur per Butler &c

•Item Elzabeth Hyggyns payeth for a barn & a garden in Wylton xviiid.

•Item the same Elzabeth payeth for land in Wylton xd.

•Item Thomas Hall payeth for a garden in Rosse to the Bysshope
of Hereford xiid.

exoneratur per Rogers &c [137]

Item a tenement in Rosse voyd payeth to the Bysshop of Herefford xiiid.

Item a tenement in Rosse in the tenure of John Harteley & payth
to the Bysshoppe of Herefford xiid. +

Item John Bell payeth for a garden to the Bysshopp vid. +

Item Robart Barber for a tenement payeth to the Bysshopp
of Herefford [138] vid. +

this in the particlers as reprised in the valure
& after also reprised againe so that the [+++]
was ?dissavid &c.

Item the same Robert payth for land to therle of Sherburye [139] id. ob. +

Item Rychard Nycholas payth for a garden to the Bysshoppe iid. +

exonerantur per Butler &c [140]

Item Ales ap Gwilem payth for a tenemente to the Bysshoppe iiiid. ob.

Item to the seyd Bysshoppe for a cheffe rent vid. +

exoneratur ut supra per Butler

•Item John Marky payeth for ii tenementes a barn & garden to
the Bysshope iiiis. id. •

•Item the same John payeth for certen landes lying in Wylton
to the Lord Grey xvid. •

exonerantur ut supra per Rogers &c [141]

Item William Chyne [142] payth for lande to the Lord Grey iiiid.

Item the same William payth for certen land in Eccleswall to
therle of Shrewesbury id. ob.

exonerantur per Jacobum Rogers & Ricardum Veale [143]

Item Thomas Somner payeth for ii acres lyeng in Wylton ^ to
the Lord Grey [^] vid.

Summa reprises xixs. ob. p:

Et sic remanet declare vi £. ~~vs. iiid~~. xviiis. viid. p:

---

[135] Wilton seems to have been meant; see below.

[136] Both the preceding payments discharged by Leighe & Vale.

[137] The three preceding payments discharged by Rogers etc.

[138] In the left-hand margin is a note at this point which extends alongside five items. To which it refers is unclear.

[139] The earl of Shrewsbury

[140] The five preceding payments discharged by Butler etc.

[141] This note refers to the two preceding items.

[142] This reads 'Thyne' but 'Chyne' is evidently meant. There may have been a copying error here at some stage.

[143] This marginal note refers to the two preceding items.

Greytree: Ross: Our Lady Service

[f. 36] **54b** The Chaunt*ery* bel*ongyng* to the Serves of O*ur* Lady in Rosse

In p*ri*mis Thomas Catter for a ten*emen*te in Rosse viis. e:

vend*itur* Tho:[me] Marshe & Rogero Will*iams*

It*em* Phelyp*p*e Harrye for the ten*emen*t of Black Worley w*ith*in the hundred of Wormelowe xiiis. iiiid. e:

vend*itur* Jo:[*hanni*] Cuper & Ric*ard*o Traver

It*em* John Hill for on*e* acre of land viiid. e: +

vend*itur* Jo:[*hanni*] Butler & Hugoni Partridge

•It*em* Harrye Garwey out of a ten*emen*te in Alton xiid.

•It*em* Rychard Dobbyns owt of a ten*emen*t in Rosse iiis. iiiid.

•It*em* Lewes Dyer payeth owt of a barn in Breke enn*er*[144] iiid.

It*em* John Harbeth for a ten*emen*te in Rosse + xiis.

vend*itur* Rogers & Veale

It*em* Wyllyam Kenett for a ten*emen*te & a garden in Rosse + xiiis. vid. e:

vend*itur* Butler

vend*itur* Jo:[*hanni*] Butler & Hugoni Partridge

•It*em* Roger Smyth out of a ten*emen*t ther iiiid. e:

It*em* Elzabeth Hagar for a garden in Rosse + xiid. ob.

vend*itur* Butler

vend*itur* eisd*em*

It*em* John Carryar for a lesowe in Wylton viiis. iiiid.

vend*itur* M*ar*she & Will*iams*

•It*em* Will*ia*m Gamon owt of hys ten*emen*te in Rosse viid.

It*em* Margery Hyggyns for a ten*emen*te in Rosse iiiis. iiiid.

It*em* Elyzabeth Grenyng for a ten*emen*te ther iiis.

•It*em* John Nourse pay*e*th owt of hys tenement + id. e: ac

•It*em* Will*ia*m Taylo*u*r owte of hys garden + iid. e:

vend*itur* Joh*an*ni Butler & Hugoni P*ar*tridge [145]

•It*em* Watter Brown pay*e*th owt of hys ten*emen*te in Edcroftes St[r]ett iid.

It*em* John Barbo*u*r for a ten*emen*t in Ov*er*hyll + vis. e: ac

It*em* Rychard Wev*er* for ~~hys~~ a ten*emen*te in Broke + vis. vid. e:

vend*itur* eisd*em* Butler & P*ar*tridge [146]

•It*em* Thomas Hall owt of a ten*emen*te iiiid.

•It*em* Will*ia*m Madocke out of a ten*emen*te in Broke End xvd. ob.

•It*em* John Yong payeth owte of hys ten*emen*te iis.

•It*em* Rychard Nycholas owt of hys ten*emen*t iiiid.

•It*em* Will*ia*m Madock out of a closse at Dode Woman + xvid. e:

vend*itur* Butler & P*ar*tridge

•It*em* Thomas Woodward out of a ten*emen*t in Rosse iiiis.

•It*em* Thomas Kart*er* payeth owt of a ten*emen*te in Rosse + ixd.

vend*itur* eisd*em* Butler & P*ar*tridge

•It*em* John Yong payeth out of a ten*emen*t in Alton iiis. ob.

vend*itur* Leighe

in p*ar*tic*ule* Edwardi Bridgec [147]

It*em* Rychard Hall [^] for [^] a ten*emen*te iiiid.

•It*em* Thomas Hall payeth owte of a house iis.

It*em* Thomas Deyken for hys ten*emen*t behynd Hyll iis. vid. e:

vend*itur* Silvestr*o* Leighe & ? Bate

•It*em* John Bayly payth out of hys ten*emen*t at Hartes xxiid.

•It*em* Will*ia*m Pukmor payth out of hys ten*emen*te iiiid.

•It*em* Rychard Nycholas payth owt of a barn xiiid. ob.

It*em* Will*ia*m Bett for a garden & acre of land in Rosse + iiiis. e:

vend*itur* Jo:[*hanni*] Butler & Hugoni P*ar*tridge

It*em* Anne Bryan for a ten*emen*t att Wyltons iis. viiid. [148]

---

[144] Could this be a misreading of 'Bicknor'?

[145] This marginal note refers to the two preceding items which are linked by a bracket and the word 'ac' (and).

[146] This marginal note refers to the two preceding items as shown by a bracket.

[147] This note in the left-hand margin is bracketed to the two preceding items.

[148] This is hard to read; 2s. 13d . would be odd, but this is the best reading.

Item Thomas Dakyn for a ten*emen*t + iiis.

vend*itur* d*ictis* Jo:[*hanni*] Butler & P*ar*tridge
in p*ar*tic*ule* Butler & P*ar*tridge vend*itur* p*er* nomen nup*er* incumbent*is*

S*umma* Cxiis. vid. p: wherof
lib*ere* xxiiiis. ad vob' iiiis. [149]
Tot*ali*s vend*itur* Butler xxxviis. ob. p:
~~This is not as it discharged ? as that it is uncertain of this ? narator~~

[f. 36v] Reddit*us* resoluti

In p*ri*mis Thomas Cator pay*e*th to the parson off Rosse xiid. e:
exoner*atur* p*er* M*ar*she & Will*iams*

Item Phelype Harry payth to the Lord Grey iiiid.
exoner*atur* p*er* Joha*nnem* Cupper & Ric*ardu*m Traver

Item John [150] payth to the Lord Grey for acre of land in Harbath Hyll +id. p:
exoner*atur* p*er* Jo:[*hannem*] Butler & Hugone*m* P*ar*tridge

Item John Harbart pay*e*th for a ten*emen*te in Rosse to ye Byshop viid.
exoner*atur* p*er* Rogers & Veale

Item Kennett pay*e*th for a ten*emen*te in Rosse to the Bysshop + xiid. e:

Item Elzabeth Aggas pay*e*th for a garde*n* to the Bysshopp*e* + ob. e:
exoner*atur* p*er* Jo:[*hannem*] Butler & Hugonem P*ar*tridge [151]

Item John Carryor payth to my Lord Grey for a leaso in Walton iiiid. e:
exoner*atur* p*er* M*ar*she & Rogers

Item Margarett Hyggyn*s* payth for a ten*emen*te in Rosse to ye Bysshope id.

It*em* Elzabeth Grenyng paith for a ten*emen*t to the seyd Bysshope id.

Item Thom*as* Deyken for a ten*emen*te in Rosse to the Bysshoppe + iid.

It*em* John Barber pay*e*th for a ten*emen*te in Rosse to the Bysshoppe + vid. e:

Item Rychard Wev*er* payth for a ten*emen*t in Rosse to ye Bysshoppe + vid. e:
exoner*antur* p*er* Jo:[*hannem*] Butler & Hugone*m* P*ar*tridge [152]

John ^ ~~Younger~~ [^] Smyth [^] Young*er*[^] pay*e*th to the seyd Bysshopp for a ten*emen*t in Rosse iiiid. ob.
exoner*atur* p*er* Leighe &c

Item Thomas Deken pay to the Bysshop for a ten*emen*t in Rosse vid.

Item Will*ia*m Bett for a ten*emen*t in Rosse to the Bysshoppe + vid.
exoner*atur* p*er* Butler &c

Item Anne Bryan for a ten*emen*t in Rosse to the Bysshoppe iid.

S*umma* rep*r*ises vis. iiid. p:
Et sic reman*et* declar*e* Cvis. iiid. e:

Greytree: Ross: St. George's Service

55 The Serves of Seynt George in Rosse [153]

In p*ri*mis Watt*er* Stokwell for a house & a orchord viis. iid. e:

Item Will*ia*m Chyn holdyth a house ii gardens & a medowe vs. vid. e:

•It*em* Harrye Logge holdyth a house xxd. e:

•It*em* Elyn Beynam for a ten*emen*te & a garden iis. iiiid. e:

•It*em* Thomas Wodward holdyth a garden att Well viiid. e:

It*em* ther ys a vacant house at Edcroft wych dyd paye iiis. iiiid. e:

•It*em* John Whytte for a howse & a garden iiis. iiiid. e:

•It*em* of Androw Wev*er* for a house & a garden iiiis. xid. e:

[f. 37] •It*em* Thomas Bayton for a house & garden iiiis. vid. e:

•It*em* off Will*ia*m Chynne for a barn & a closse vs. e:

•It*em* Rychard Nycoll for a barn & a acre off lande iiis. vd. e:

---

[149] The meaning of this line is wholly unclear.

[150] This item is linked with the next by a bracket. 'John' is therefore John Harbart.

[151] This marginal note refers to both the preceding items.

[152] This marginal note appears to have been linked by bracket to the two preceding items and then by extension of the bracket to the item before them, 'Thomas Deyken'.

[153] This list contains several names and other detail in such brief form that it seems likely that they were badly copied (missing out names and words) from another document.

Item of Thomas Cater for a barn vs. iiiid.

venditur Tho*me* Mar*she* & Roger*o* Will*iams*

Item the same Thomas for a howse & a garden in Rosse viiis. ixd. e:

•Item John Yonge a howse & a garden xs. iiiid. e:

•Item Will*iam* ap Jevan for a howse xiiiis. viiid. e:

•Item Thomas holdythe iii acres of land in Alver Hyll xviid. e:

•Item Rychard Nycoll*es* payth yerely owt of hys house iiiid. e:

•Item Rychard Daves holdyth in Rosse iiis. viiid. e:

•Item Will*iam* Belamye [154] acre of land Polefeld xiid. e:

•Item Amend a acre of land iiiid. e:

•Item John Taylo*ur* for a howse & a garden in Rosse iis. xd. e:

•Item Will*iam* for a howse & a closse iiis. e:

•Item John Belamye for a acre of land in Pyryfeld viiid. e:

Item a garden in Edcroft Strette iis. e:

Item a lesowe in the tenure of Will*iam* Dewe the rent [155] ~~xvid~~. e:

cancell*atur* quo*minusque* melius ex*aminatu*r p:

vendit*ur* ist*i* xvid. Rogers &c

Summa iiii £. ~~xviis. vid~~. xvis. iid.

Tot*um* ist*ius* cant*arie* vendit*ur* Rogers & Veale except*ive* vs. iiiid.

in te*nura* Thome Catter p*ro* uno orreo

Reddit*us* resoluti

In p*r*imis Will*iam* Stowell payth to the p*ar*son of Rosse for a tenement and a garden vid.

Item Will*iam* Chyne to the Bysshop of Heref*ord* for ii gardens & a medowe vid.

Item Harry Logg*er* payth for a ten*emen*te to the Bysshoppe iid.

Item Elzabeth Beynaham pay*e*th to the Bysshop for a ten*emen*t & garden iiiid.

Item Thom*as* Woodward pay*e*th ^ to the Bysshope [^] for a ten*emen*te & a garden vid.

Item ther ys a howse vacant that pay*e*th ^ to the Bysshope [^] vid.

It*em* John Hyett pay*e*th to the seyd Bysshope for a house & a garden vid.

Item Androwe Loyd pay*e*th for a house & a garden to ye Bysshope xid.

Item Thomas Bayton for a ten*emen*t & a garden to the Bysshope vid

Item Will*iam* Chynn for a barne & a closse to the Bysshoppe vid.

Item Rychard Nycoll*es* pay*e*th to the p*ar*son of Rosse for a barn & ii plockes iiiid.

It*em* Thom*as* Cater for a barn & ii plockes to the seyd p*ar*son iiiid.

exon*eratur per* ~~Roger~~ M*ar*she & Will*iams*

Item of [156]

[f. 37v] Item Izott Tom*mes* payth to the p*ar*son for a house & a garden ixd.

Item John Yonge smyth pay*e*th to the p*ar*son for a house & garden ixd.

It*em* the same John pay*e*th to the Lord of Shrewesbery for a medo plock viiid.

Item Will*iam* ap Jau*a*n pay*e*th to the p*ar*son for a medo & acre of land xiid.

It*em* Rychard Daves payth to the Bysshoppe for a house vid.

It*em* John Taylo*ur* pay*e*th for a house & a garden to the Bysshop iid.

It*em* Will*iam* Taylo*ur* pay*e*th to the Lord of Shrewesbury for a ten*emen*te att Pengelthlye iid.

S*umma* rep*r*ises ixs. vid. p:

exon*erantur per* p*er*quisit*ores*

ex*ceptive* iiiid. p*ro* orreo in te*nura* Tho*me* Catter

Et sic remanet declare iiii £. ~~xiid~~. ~~viiis.~~ vis. vid. p:

~~no*tatur*~~

---

[154] The document says here (and 4 lines below) 'Lelanye'. It appears to be a bad copying of the name 'Belamy or Bellamy', a family resident in Ross at the time.

[155] See also section 90c.

[156] This seems to be a line begun but not followed through, presumably the opening words repeated on the next page.

Greytree: Ross: Obits

56 The Rent Roule of the Obyte Money

In p*ri*mis off John Hachat for rent of a shop that belongyth to the churche — iis

It*e*m of Watter Stowell for the rent of a medo in Wylton — iis. viiid. e:

It*e*m of Anne Ruddall wedowe for the rent of a medowe — iiis.

vend*itur* Jacobo Rogers & Veale [157]

It*e*m of Watter a Gw*i*l*y*m for a rent out of a ten*emen*te in Rosse — vis. viiid.

It*e*m of Rychard Nycoll*e*s for the rent of a medow Michaelm*as* Medo — iiiis. e:

vend*itur* eisd*e*m Rogers & Veale

S*umma* — xviiis. iiiid. p:

Greytree: Weston-under-Penyard: Our Lady Service

57 The Serves of Our Ladye w*ith*in the Churche of Weston

•In p*ri*mis Anne Ruddall pay*e*th owte off a ten*emen*te in Kyngeston the rent off — iiis. iiiid. e:

•It*e*m John Hart payth out of acre of freland — iiiid. e:

•It*e*m John Brugman payth out of hys freland & hys cosyns called Whete Land — xxd. e:

•It*e*m Thomas Howe payth owte yerelye of of hys freland in Weston — xd. e:

•It*e*m Thomas Dun*n*e pay*e*th owt off hys freland — viiid. e:

•It*em* Robart Howe pay*e*th owt off hys fre land in Brodfeld — vid. e:

vend*untur* Ja:[*cobo*] Rogers & Veale

It*em* John Smyth holdyth a feld ther — xvid.

vend*itur* Joh*anni* Thumes

•It*e*m Thom*as* Rugge payth out of hys freland in Walton — xiid. e:

vend*itur* ut sup*ra*

Item Thomas Addes for a medowe — xvs. viiid. e:

vend*itur* Jo:[*hanni*] Thumes

Item the same Thomas for iiii acres of land — viiid.

vend*itur* Joh*anni* Thu[*mes]

[f. 38] •It*e*m Will*ia*m Taylo*ur* for on*e* medowe — vs. e:

•It*e*m Harrye Rugge the yong*er* for a medowe & c*er*ten land*e*s — ixs. viiid. e:

•It*e*m the same Harrye for a closse — iis. e:

•It*e*m John Harres for ii acres of medowe & iiii of errable — viiis. e:

vend*untur* Joh*anni* Tumkes &c [158]

•It*e*m John Bruggeland pay*e*th owt of hys free land in Walton — iis. iid. e:

vend*itur* Joc:[*obo*] Rogers & Veale

Item John Rugge for c*er*ten landes — xviis. e:

Item John Gorwey for acre of medo & a p*ar*cell of lande — vis. viiid. e:

vend*itur* Jo:[*hanni*] Thumes

•It*e*m John Tom*m*es pay*e*th yerely oute of hys fre lande — xxiid. e:

vend*itur* eisd*e*m Rogers & Veale

Item Watter Rugge holdyth by copye a chamber & a garde*n* — xxd. e:

vend*itur* Jo:[*hanni*] Thumes

•It*e*m the same Watter payth out of hys frehouse in Ponshyll — ixd. e:

vend*itur* ut sup*ra* [159]

• Item Harrye Ruge for a masuage & c*er*ten land*e*s — iiis. e:

vend*itur* Jo:[*hanni*] Thumes

Item Thomas Lloyd holdyth xxiiii acres of land in Hally — iiis. iiiid. e:

vend*itur* Joh*anni* Thumes

•It*em* Rych*ard* Walwyn esquyer payth out of hys freland in Ponshyll — iiiid. e:

•It*em* Harry Hoggys of Bylmyll pay*e*th owt of a dole of freland — iiiid. e:

vend*untur* eisd*e*m Rogers & Veale [160]

It*em* John Ruge of Castell holdythe c*er*ten land*e*s by indenture — iiiis. vid. e:

vend*itur* Joh*anni* Thomes

---

157 This marginal note is linked by bracket to the two preceding items.

158 The preceding 4 items linked by this bracketed note.

159 In fact this refers to Rogers & Veale, which was the previous sale noted in the margin on this, the right-hand, side of the page.

160 The two preceding items linked by bracket to this marginal note.

•Item Wil*lia*m Ruge of Kyngeston pay*e*th yerely owt of a cha*m*ber viiid. e:
vend*itur* d*ictis* Rogers & Veale
Item a mese place that the p*r*iest dwellyth in iiis. iiiid. e:
vend*itur* Thom*e* M*ar*she & Roger*um* Will*iams*
~~no*tatur* mese voc*atur* the P*r*iestes Howse~~
~~ad iiis. iiid. p*er* an*num* rem*an*et in man*u*~~
~~R*egis* nondu*m* vend*itur* resid*uum* vend*itur*~~
~~Ja:[*cobo*] Rogers & Ric*ardo* Veale~~
Item Nycholas Coocke a mese & app*er*ten*a*unces viiis. e:
vend*itur* Joh*anni* Thume

lib*ere* xiiiis. vd.[161]
ad ? vob' iiii £. ixs. xd.
Summa Ciiiis. iiid. p:

Reddit*us* resolut*i*
In p*ri*mis payd owt of Basshames Medowe vis. viiid.
~~exoner*andum* p*er* Rogers & Veale~~
exon*eratur* p*er* Jo*hann*em Thume
Item payd owt of the seyd medowe to ye late Abotte of Flaxley xiid.
extinguit*ur*
Item John Ruge pay*e*th to the lord of the Lee viiis. iiiid.
exon*eratur* ut sup*ra*
exon*eratur* p*er* eadem Joh*ann*em Thume
Item p*ai*d out of the me*n*cyon house that ye p*r*iest dwell in to
the Lord off Shrewesberye iiiid.
exon*eratur* p*er* Tho*mam* M*ar*she & Roge*rum* Willia*m*z
exon*eratur* p*er* d*ictu*m Roge*rs*
It*em* Will*ia*m Ruge payth of the p*r*iestes house to the Lord of
Shrewesbery iid.
ut sup*ra*
exon*eratur* p*er* dic*tum* Joh*ann*em Thume
S*umma* rep*ri*ses xvis. vid. p:
Et sic remane*t* declare iiii £. viis. ~~viiid~~. ixd.[162] p:

Greytree: Weston-under-Penyard: Lamp and Lights

[f. 38v] **58** Lampe Lyghtes ther
In p*ri*mis of John Smyth di*midie* acre of lande iid. e:
Item off Swayn di*midie* acre called the Lamp Hey viiid. e:
Item off Thomas on*e* acre of land in Lamp Heye viiid. e:
vend*untur* Jacobo Rogers & Veale
S*umma* xviiid. p:

Greytree: Linton: Our Lady Service

59 The Serves of O*u*r Ladye in Lynton
In p*ri*mis of Harrye ap Adam holdyth a mesuag*e* & ii yard land*es* Lvis. id. e:
Item of Roger a Goddeshalf holdyth a mesuage & other landes viiis.
•Item Rychard Ellesmere holdyth a mesuag*e* & c*er*ten land*es* viiis.
vend*itur* Jac:[*obo*] Rogers & Veale
Item James Pyper holdyth c*er*ten land*es* by Dedeland iis. iid. e:
It*em* John Taylo*u*r holdyth a mesuage & xviii acres ~~& above of land~~ ixs. viid. e:
Item Thomas Walker holdyth a p*ar*cell of lande iiiid. e:
Item John How holdyth vi acres of land in Bromfeld iis. e:
It*em* Thom*as* Phelyp*es* payeth owt of hys freland in Bromfeld xviiid. e:
Item Will*iam* Ellye holdyth a medowe lying above Ruddalles Halles iis. e:
Item the p*r*iestes house lying in Lyntons Strette iis. iid. e:
Item Thomas Ellesmore holdyth ii acres of land viiid. e:

161 The meaning of this and the next entry is unclear; the two represent a breakdown of the total.
162 This total is also shown by an auditor' use grid in the left-hand margin.

Item John Berch holdyth ii acres called Lady Plucke xviiid. e:
Item Nicholas Jonys for certen lond [163] ~~vis. viiid.~~

cancellatur quominusque melius examinatur

venduntur Ja:[cobo] Rogers & Ricardo Veale [164]

Summa ~~Cs. viiid~~. iiii £. xiiiis.

venduntur Jacobo Rogers & Ricardo Veale

Redditus resoluti

In primis payd to therle off Shrewesbury for a tenemente in the holdyng of John Taylour vis. iiid.
Item payd to the seyd Erle a cheff rent vis. viiid.
Item payd yerely to the heyres of Rychard Rudhsll out of the forseyd farme of Harrye Uppadam ixs. iiiid.

exonerantur per Rogers & Veale

Summa reprises xxiis. iiid. p:
Et sic remanet declare ~~Lxxviiis. vd~~. Lxxis. xd. p:

Greytree: Mordiford

[f. 39] **60**. The Landes that belongyth to Mordyfford

•In primis for certen landes in the tenure of Roger Herefford viiid. for ii gese & dimidie libra comyn viiis. viiid. dewe to Humffrey Conesby esquyer for a cheffe rent xs. iiiid. e: e:
•Item of William Colyer for certen [165] that he holdyth vis. xd. e: e:
•Item for certen tenementes in the tenure of Thomas Archard a pound of comyn dew to the seyd Roger Hereford for a cheff rent over & bysydes iiis. iiiid. dewe to Sir John Prece knyght for a lyke cheffe rent vis. iid. e: e:
•Item certen landes in the tenure of Rychard Mercer over & besides vs. for cheff rent dewe to the kynges maieste as parcell of the possessyons of the late priorye of Shene over & besydes id. for a cheffe rent dewe to Roger Bodnaham gent. over & besydes xixd. for a cheff rent dew to the seyd Roger Herefford xviiis. iiiid. e: e:
•Item a certen tenemente in the tenure of Davyd Thomas over & besydes ixd. ob. dewe to the prebendaryes of Herefford vis. viiid. e: e:
•Item for certen landes in the tenure of Walter Hoggys over & besydes iis. vid. for a cheffe rent & over & besydes iis. vid. dewe to the seyd Humfrey Connynsbe esquyer iiiis. e: e:

venduntur Rogero Hareford & Jo:[hanni] Prediaux [166]

Item for certen land in the tenure of Rychard Tomkyns over & besides xiid. dewe to the seyd Roger Herefford viis.

remanet in manu Regis

Item Humfrey Conynsby esquyer for a yerely rent goyng out of a closse called Wattes Closse lying in Priours Frome xiid. e: e:
Item a certen howse with a closse & a dove house wherin ~~the sayd Sir Davyd~~ ^ Thomas [^] dwellyth over & besides xiid. for a cheffe rent dewe to the sayd Roger Herefford xis. iiiid. e: e:

venduntur prefatis Rogero Hareford & Jo:[hanni] Prediaux

Summa Lxxis. viiid. p:

Redditus resoluti

In primis payd to Master Herefford for a quytt rent viiid.
Item to Master Herefford for a cheffe rent xiid.
Item payd to Master Connynsby viiis. viiid.
Item to Master Pryce iiis.
Item to the kynges maiestye baylys iiis. viiid.
Item to the kynges maieste ^ bayles ther [^] vs.
[f. 39v] Item to Master Bodnaham id.

---

[163] In a different hand. A marginal note, struck through, in section 76 and also section 90a refers to this item.
[164] This note in the left-hand margin refers to all the items in the above list, bracketed together.
[165] A word missing; proof that this is to some extent a copied document.
[166] This left hand marginal note brackets all the above items.

Item to Master Herefford xixd.
Item to the prebend*aries* of Herefford ixd. ob.
Item to M*aste*r Cony*n*sbe iis. vid.
Item to Roger Herefford xiid.

tota exonerantur per perquisitores

S*umma* rep*rises* xxviis. xid. ob. p:
Et sic reman*et* declar*e* xliiis. viiid. ob.

Greytree: Mordiford: Lamp lights

61. Lampe lyghtes
In p*ri*mis on*e* acre of land in the tenure of Rychard Tydnor iiiid.
Item on*e* acre of land lying in Kackleys Feld to me*n*teyn a lampe iid.
S*umma* vid. p:

Greytree: Much Marcle: Our Lady Service

62. The Land*es* that belongyth to the Serves of O*ur* Lady in Much*e* M*ar*kell
In p*ri*mis Fowke Hoper xviiis. e:
Item Thomas Appowell xs. e:

vend*untur* Wil*lel*mo Winlove & Ric*ard*o Feild [167]

Item Rychard Gamond vis. viiid. e:
Item Will*ia*m Brygge xxiis.

ist*ius* vis. viiid. vend*itur* Silvestr*o* Leigh &c [168]
in man*u* R*egis* [169]

Item John ap Thomas iis. viiid. e:

vend*itur per* nomen Thome Tomey [170]

Item Thomas Turno*ur* iis. e:
Item Thomas a Brygge xiid. e:
Item John Kyft iiis. e:
Item Harrye May iiid. e:

notatur in p*ar*ticu*l*is iiiid.

Item Hew Wyll*ia*ms xiid. e:
Item Will*ia*m Colyar iiiid. e:
Item Davyd Lane viiid. e:
Item Tho:[*mas*] Dyke iid. e:
Item Robart Clerke iis. e:

vend*untur* eisd*em* Winlove & Feld [171]

S*umma* Lxixs. ixd. p:
wherof

[f. 40] Redd*itus* resolut*i*
In p*ri*mis payd to the Quenes grace xiiid. ob.
Item payd to my Lord Grey for cheffe rent iiis. i l*ibra* of pep*er* iiis.
S*umma* rep*ri*ses iiiis. id. ob. p:
Et sic reman*et* declar*e* Lxvs. viid. ob. p:

Greytree: Much Marcle: Obit

63. A Obytt in the P*ar*yssh of Moch Markell
In p*ri*mis a obett menteyned ther on John Walle iis.
S*umma* iis. p:

---

167 Both the preceding items bracketed together to this note.
168 'Silvestr Leigh &c' is written into the margin of the facing page.
169 The preceding two items are linked to this marginal note.
170 This note in the left-hand margin relates to this item, but the bracket linking the rest of the items seems to extend as far as here too.
171 This left hand marginal note is linked by a bracket, whose ends do not curl inwards, to all the items from (and perhaps including) John ap Thomas to Robert Clerke.

Greytree: Upton Bishop: Obit

64. A Obyttes in the Parysh of Upton Bysshoppe
In p*ri*mis acre of medowe called Harnett*es* Medo w*ith* ii acres of errable land in the tenure of Rob*er*t Home gevyn by one Reynold to the meyntenaunce off one obytte iiiis. e:

vend*itu*r Reve & Johnson

Redd*itus* resolut*i*
Item payd owte off the same xxd. e:

exon*eratur* p*er* eosdem
And so remayne clere iis. iiiid. e:

Greytree: Upton Bishop: Church Repairs

64a P*a*roch*ia* de Upton Bisshoppe

no*tatu*r [172]

In p*ri*mis xii acres of errable land called Cote Land in the tenure of Thomas Gatcom*be* gevyn toward*es* the rep*ar*acyons of the churche iiis. e:

vend*itur* eisdem Reve & Johnson

Redd*itus* resoluti
In p*ri*mis payd owt of the same iid. ob. e:

exon*eratur* ex' p*er* eosdem
And so remayn clere iis. ixd. ob. e:

Greytree: Hope Mansell: Lamp Light

65. Hope Maunsell P*ar*ysh Lampe Lyght
In p*ri*mis ii acres of errable land in the tenure of Thomas Blast toward the fyndyng of one lampe viiid. e:

Greytree: How Caple: Lamplights

66. How Capell P*ar*ysh Lamplyghtes
In p*ri*mis on*e* acre of errable land in the tenure of John Welsh to the menten*a*unce of a lyght iiiid. e:

vend*untur* Jacob*o* Rogers & Vea[*le] [173]

Greytree: Woolhope: Lamp

67. The Parishe of Wolehope a Lamplyght [174]
Item an annuall rent going out of a mese and certeyn land lying in the said p*ar*ish iis. viiid. e:

Greytree: Walford: Our Lady Service

[f. 40v] **68** The Land*es* & Tenement*es* belon[g]yng to O*u*r Lady Serves in Walford
In p*ri*mis Edmond Eme holdyth v acres off errable land at Howle by rent by yere iis.
Item Watter Farmer holdyth a mese & c*e*rten land*es* called Porters nowe in the tenure of John M*ar*kye the rent by yere xs. vid. e:
Item John Hyett holdyth a mesuage called Mawde Monnys by rent by yere vs. e:
Item Thomas Morton holdyth a mesuage called Whytwall by rent by yere xiis. e:

vend*untur* Jacob*o* Rogers & Ric*ardo* Veale [175]

Item Thomas Cryll holdyth a mesuage called Chases Howse w*ith* certen land*es* by rent by yere viiis.

vend*itur* p*r*efat*is* Rogers & Veale

Item the same Thomas for cheffe rent*es* iiis. iiiid. e:

vend*itur* p*r*efat*is* Ja:[*cobo Rogers*] & Ric*ardo* [*Veale*]

---

[172] This instruction draws attention to the fact that this set of Upton Bishop items had been missed.
[173] Both the Hope Mansell and the How Caple properties were sold to Rogers and Veale.
[174] Although numbered in the sequence of the original, this paragraph is written in a different hand from the rest of the page and has been squeezed in at the foot of the page.
[175] The marginal note is bracketed to the preceding three items.

Item Rychard Harrys for cheffe rent*es* out of hys fre land*es* in Walford by rent by yere xxd.
It*em* John Morton holdyth a cotage by indenture lying in the Soundyng by rent by yere + iis. iiiid. e:
vend*itur* Joh*anni* Butler & Hugoni P*ar*tridge
It*em* John Shrewesbyry for a p*ar*cell off land att Colbery vid.
S*umma* xlvs iiiid. e:

Redd*itus* resolut*us*
In p*ri*mis payd owt of a mese & c*er*ten land*es* called Porters to the Erle of Saloppe xiid. e:
It*em* payd owt of a mesuage called Mawde Monnys to Thomas Kyrle gentylman iis. e:
It*em* payd owt of a mese called Whytwall to ~~Watter a Gwyllym gentylman~~ [^] therle of Shrewesbury [^] xiid. e:
S*umma* rep*r*ises iiiis. p:
exon*erantur per* Jacob*um* Rogers & Ric*ardu*m Veale
Et sic reman*et* declar*e* xlis. iiiid. e:

Greytree Totals

[68a] S*umma* totall of the sayde Ch*a*untres ye rep*ri*ses not deducted xxxix £. iiiis. iiid. ob. p:
Rep*ri*ses yerlye Cxis. vid. e: p:
And so rem*ains* finis xxxii £. xiis. ixd. ob. p: e:[176]

[f. 41] Hundred of Wormelowe

Wormilow: St. Weonards: Obits

69 Saynt Wanyard*es* Obytes
In p*ri*mis vi acres off errable land whiche Davyd Come gave for to have a yerely obytt iiis. iiiid.
It*em* ~~Raynald Dewevered kept a~~ yerely obytt for Thomas Devawer [177] goyng owt of a certen closse called Henny Seyn xxd.
It*em* Thom*as* Robert ap Gwillym do kepe yerely for the soule of Robart ap Gw*i*llym w*ith* the rent of a c*er*ten lande lyeng in Lagmo*n*ck*es* Feld iiis. vid.
Obyttes m*emorandum*
S*umma* viiis. vid. p:

Wormilow: Ballingham: Anniversary

70 The P*a*rysh of Bellyngham
In p*ri*mis Will*ia*m Scudamo*ur* of Bellyngham gave c*er*ten land*es* in the p*a*ryssh of Hentland to the valure ^ to the use of a lampe [^] off xiiiis. by yere in the teno*ur* of Elzabeth Jones [178] ~~xiiiis~~. xs. e:
vend*itur* Thome Hungate & Aynsworth
in l*itte*ris paten*tibus* ad usu*m* anniv*er*sar*ii*
S*umma* xs. ~~id~~. p:

Wormilow: Dewsall: Lamp

71 P*ar*ochia de Dewswall
In p*ri*mis a ^ pece [^] of land lying in the Hale Joyne to Haywod geven to mayntayn a lampe nowe in the tenure of John Parle xvid. e:
vend*itur* eisdem Hungate & Aynsworth
S*umma* xvid. p:

---

[176] The shillings and pence are written on the facing page. The arithmetic (and the net total) is incorrect. The net total should be £33 12s. 9½d. But the sum of the Greytree individual net totals is £32 16s. 10½d.
[177] This name is obviously a misreading (from an antecedent document) of the name of Thomas David Vaure, which would have been written 'Thomas Dd Vaure'.
[178] See also section 90d.

Wormilow: Kings Caple: Obit

72 Kynges Capull Obytt
In p*ri*mis John Cockes deceassed gave a closse to the fyndyng off
a obytte nowe in the holdyng of Thomas Cole xvd. p:
vend*itur* Jacobo Rogers & Veale
S*umma* xvd. e:

Wormilow: Dewchurch: Andrew Voyle's Obit

73 Dewchurche
In p*ri*mis ii closes on*e* called Crosseyket & the other Trybellet
in the tenure of Rychard Vaughan for a obytt for Androwe
? ~~Boil~~ Voyle iiis. vid. e:
vend*itur* ~~ut supra~~ di*c*tis Hungate & Aynsworthe
S*umma* iiis. vid. e:

Wormilow: Goodrich: a Mass & Lamps

74 Goddrygge
In p*ri*mis a yerely rent owt of the land*es* off Henyon to say a masse xvd.
vend*itur* ~~ut supra~~ eisd*em*
S*umma* xvd. e:
~~No*tatur* to se the valewe hereof before the dischardge~~
[f. 41v] Lampe In p*ri*mis ii acres & a halfe off errable lande in the tenure
of John Smyth to menteyn a lampe xd. e:
S*umma* xd.
Lampe In p*ri*mis iiiid. by the yere out of a medow called Luckes
Medow p*ar*cell of the land*es* of Thomas Edward iiiid.
S*umma* iiiid. e:
S*umma* [*blank*]

Wormilow: ? Michaelchurch and Tretire: Obits

75 Wormelowe Obytes Ther
In p*ri*mis goyng owte of the capytall messe off Thomas Abrall [179] to
kepe a obytte yerely iis. xid.
Item one yerely obitt kept yerely Thom*as* Abrall w*ith*in the p*ar*ishe
churche aforsaid [180] xxd.
[*Total*] iiiis. viid. e:
vend*untur* Jacobo Rogers & Veale

Wormilow: Whitchurch: Stipendiary Priest

76 Wychechurche a Stypendary P*r*iest ther
In p*ri*mis a stypendary p*r*iest founde ther owte off c*er*ten land*es* in
the tenure of Thom*as* Turnor & other Lxs. e:
vendit*ur* eisd*em* Rogers & Veale
M*emorandum* in the p*ar*ticler*s* of the survei made to the p*ur*chaser
ther is conteinid more then here charged xs. p*er* ann*um* for a
mes*e* & xviii acres of arrable & pasture let to Thom*as* Apowell
Ideo ?ayd &c
wherof: Repr*is*es
In p*ri*mis payd owt of the same to the lord off Shrewesburye iiis.
Item to the sayd lord iis.
• Item to Thomas Hunteley xiid.
• Item to Thomas Appowell id. ob.
• Item to Robart Taylo*ur* viiid.
• Item to Will*iam* Cotta vd.
• Item to Robart Phelpott vd.
• Item to John Jenyn id. ob.
S*umma* repr*is*es viis. ixd. p:

---

179 Thomas Abrall was the chief resident of the parish of Michaelchurch and Tretire (*Herefordshire Taxes*, 213).
180 This item written in a different and more hurried hand.

Et sic reman*et* declar*e*   Liis. iiid.

M*emorandum* that where it dothe apere upon the p*re*sentment of Lynton aforseyd that a certeyn*e* pece of land being in thand*e*s of Nicholas Jones of the yerely value of vis. viiid. in the forsaid chauntre chargdged The chauntre prest therof did put in ye same upon very malice and the said Nicholas dyd nev*er* paye the same as he ~~suppos*eth*~~ supposed upon his othe [181]

Wormilow: Bridstow: Obits

[f. 42] **76a** [182] Obyttes in the Parishe of Brydstowe
In p*ri*mis a c*er*ten closse called Robart Daves Closse lying in Asshe w*ith*in the P*ar*ysshe of Brydstowe gevyn by Thomas Long to menteyn an obytt for hym & hys frend*e*s by the rent by the yere   vid. e:
vend*itur* Rogers & Veale
It*em* the stipendary preste ~~gyven~~ founded by the Lord Grey in the Castell of Wilton which hath ~~yt~~ ben p*ai*d owt of the parsonage of Brydstowe   iiii £.
[*Total*]   iiii £ vid. p:

Wormilow: Peterstow: Lights

77 Peterstowe Lyghtes
In p*ri*mis on*e* acre off errable land gevyn for the mayntena*u*nce off a lyght in the tenure off Thomas Vaughan   viiid. e:
vend*itur* Thome Hungate & Aynsworth

Wormilow: Sellack: Obits

78 P*ar*ochia de Sellacke
In p*ri*mis iii yerely obytes meynteyned by Thomas More clarke   ~~xxid.~~   xxvis. viiid. e:
wherof: To pore people in the p*ar*ishe of Hentland, Kyng Capell & in the same p*ar*ish   xxs. e:
And so remayn*s*   vis. viiid. e:
M*emorandum* to staie the p*ar*ticlers hereof if this p*ar*cell be sued for till the returne of John ? Robertes ?who ys [183] ten*a*unt therof

Wormilow: Little Birch: Obits

79. Perochia de Lyttell Berche Obyttes
In p*ri*mis that on*e* Phelyp Drome [184] holdyth c*er*ten land*e*s of hys gyfte lying in the seyd p*ar*yshe to fynd a obytte   vs. vid. e:
vend*itur* Jacobo Rogers & Ric*ardo* Veale

Wormilow: Welsh Newton: Lamplight

80. The Parishe of Welshe Newton Lamplyght
Item a mese & certeyn land lying in Welshenewton aforsaid   viiis. e:

Wormilow Totals

[80a] Summ*m* totall of the saide hundreth the rep*r*ises not deducted   x £. xiis. xid. e: p:
Rep*r*ises yerly   xxviis. ixd. e: p:
cu*m* xxs. in elemos*inis*
Amd so rem*ains*   ix £. vs. iid. [185] p: e:

---

[181] See section 90a. This entire paragraph has been struck through, but for reasons of editorial clarity that has not been shown in this edition.

[182] The original numbering has gone awry. There are two blocks of detail called '76'. Here we distinguish betwen them by adding the suffix 'a' to the second one.

[183] The three words before the footnote no. were written faintly and across the next title. 'Roberts' may be the surname; a John Roberts lived in Hentland (M.A.Faraday, *Herefordshire Taxes in the Reign of Henry VIII*, 349)

[184] There is no sign of anyone called 'Drome' in Herefordshire at the time, but a Philip Come or Combe lived in Little Birch in the 1540s, (*Herefordshire Taxes*, 218, 393). This is evidence that the document was copied from another document and that a capital 'C' was mistaken for a 'D'.

[185] The net total after taking account of the 20s. paid in alms is £8 5s. 2d.

[f.42v] Hundred de Webbetre

Webtree: Dorston: Chantry

81. The Landes that belongyth to the Chauntery within the Parysshe Cherch of Dorston

In primis Thomas Parteruge holdyth a tenemente & a garden	xxixs. xid.
Item Thomas Weston holdyth iiii acres off medowe	viis. xd.
Item Elyzabeth Vaughan holdyth ii acres of medowe & other off errable lande	iiis. iid.
Item William John Rees holdyth one acre of medowe & a quarter of a acre of errable land	iis. xid.
~~Item William John Rees &~~ Rychard Hyggyn holdyth one acre of medow & iiii acres of errable lande +	xiid. e:
Item Howell ap Thomas a plocke of wood & iiii acres of errable land +	xvid. e:
Item of Margarett ap Jenkyn a howse & a garden +	xiid. e:
Item ~~William~~ John Williams iii acres of errable land + ~~vid.~~	xiid. e:
Item Myles Taylor one tenement +	iis. e:
Item Thomas ap Hoell for iiii acres of errable land	iis.
Item Phelyp Smyth for a closse	vid.
Item William a Gannell ii acres errable & a plock of medo +	xiiiid. e:
Item John Watter one tenemente	iis. id.
Item Margarett Tewe a nother tenemente	iis.
Item Thomas a Whytney a tenemente	iis.
Item Thomas Butler a tenemente	iis.
Item Thomas Baker a tenement	iis.
Item Thomas Watter for annuyte +	xiid. e:
Item Myles ap Davyd annuyte	xiid.
Item Thomas ap John	iid.
Item John Hoell	ixd.
Item Maud Taylour	vid.
Item Thomas Taylour	iiiid.
Item Margery Rosser	iiiid.
Item of John Lewes for ii ~~tenement~~ acres lond	vid.
Item a tenement in the tenur of Thomas John	xvid.
Summa	Lxixs. xd. p:

exoneratur e: p: [186]

Notatur viiis. vid. per annum prout annotatur infra venditur inter alios Jo:[hanni] Dodington generoso & heredibus suis per litteras patentes datas xvi° Decembris anno iii^io Regis Edwardi VI^ti exitas a festo Annunciationis ultimo tenendum in socagio ut de manerio de Estgrenewich in comitatu Kantii absque prima inde reservatas ac per ipsum alienatur Johanni Walwine & Margarete uxori eius ac heredibus & assignatis ipsius Jo:[hannis] in perpetuum per eius cartam datam xvii die Decembris Anno predicto

Audita ostenca & examinata [187]

[f. 43] Reprises

In primis payd owte of the same to Syr Mychaell Lyster knyght	viiis. vid. e:
Summa declare remanet	Lxis. iiiid. e:

Webtree: Madley: Our Lady Chantry

82 The Landes that Belong to the Chauntery of Our Lady in the Church of Madley

• In primis Watter Lewellyn for a mese & a tenemente	xiiis. iiiid. e:
• Item of Margarett Hurley wedowe	iiiis. e:
• Item of Kateryn Russell wedowe for a cotage	iiis. iiiid. e:
• Item of William ap Thomas for iii acres of errable land	
oon busshell & a pecke of whete	xd.
& a busshell of otes	iiid.
• Item Thomas Tomkyns for the furme of Lytle Bromton	xxxviiis. iiiid. e:

---

[186] The three preceding marks are in the margin opposite Myles Taylor and Thomas ap Hoell.

[187] This note is in the left hand margin next to the last 16 items in the list; it is not apparent whether it refers to all or some of the sixteen.

- Item off Rychard Gullyfer for xii acres of errable lande
  iiii busshells of whete — iis. viiid.
- of the same Rychard for a lesowe called Seynt Marye Hayes — xxd. e:
- Item of Anne ap Yevan wedowe for ii acres & a halfe of
  errable lande — xd. e:
- Item of Laurens of Wellyngton for xvi acres off errable lande
  v busshelles & a pecke of whete — iiis. vid.
  v busshelles of otes — xvd.
- Item the same Laurens for a lesowe — xviid.
- for Watter Wenland for xxxix acres off errable lande — iiiis. iiid.
  xiii busshelles of whete — viiis. viiid.
  & xiii bushels of otes — iiis. iiid.
- Item Thomas Mathowes for vi acres of errable land — iis. viiid.
- Item of John Medmore for one halfe yard land
  iiiis. iiid. [188] ~~vii~~ ^ xvii [^] busshelles & a pecke of whete — xis. vid.
  xiiii busshelles of otes — iiis. vid.
- Item John Hopkyns for viii acres off errable lande
  ii busshelles & a pecke of whete — xviiid.
  ii busshelles of otes — vid.
- Item William Bell for a acre of errable land — iiiid. e:

Summa Lxxs. iid. p: [189]

Summa Totall of the Whete & Ottes iiii/xx i busshell
yt is to saye
Whette xliii bushelles — xxviiis. viiid. e:
Ottes xxxviii [*busshells] — viiis. xd. e:
Totalis ottes and wheat Lxxviii bushelles [190]

[f. 43v] The summ of the busshelles off wheate
payd yerely ys xliii busshelles
att viiid. the busshell — xxviiis. viiid.
The summ of the busshelles of otes
ys xxxv busshelles at ~~the bushel~~
iiid. le bushell — viiis. ixd.
xxxviis. vd.

Summa ~~clare~~ totall of the Rentes
wheat & ottes prised — Cviis. viid. p: [191]
?tamdiu de redditu ?quamdiu de grano [192]

wherof: Reprises
In primis Morgan Llewellen [193] payeth owte of hys mese to chapter
off Herefford — vs. iiiid.
Item Margerett Huett for a cotage to the sayd chapter — iid.
Item Katryn Russell for a cotage to the seyd chapter — iiiid.
Item Thomas Tomkyns for a farm payeth to Thomas Dansye — iiis. iiiid.
Item of the seyd Thomas for Seynt Marye Heyes to the lord
of Kynstone — viiid.
Item Rychard Golefer for xii acres of errable land seyd chapter — iiiid. ob.
Item Rychard Golefer for a pasture to Sir Mychaell Lyster knyght — xiiiid.
Item for a lesowe & xvi acres in the tenure of Laurens Wellyngton
to the seyd chapter — xviid.
Item Walter Wenland for xxxix ti acres of errable land to the seyd Dene — xviiid.

---

188 This, although not struck through, seems to be the value of the 7 bushells subsequently struck through. even though the unit value is not quite the same..
189 This is the total of the rents other than the grain rents.
190 The total of the wheat and oats in the valuations is 43 bushels of wheat and 35 bushels of oats, so the marginal note is correct.
191 The total of the money and grain rents.
192 Assuming that my reading of the abbreviated words is correct, I am indebted to Murray Glover for this translation: " The rent is paid so long as there is grain".
193 Some Christian names in the reprises differ from those in the main list; it is unclear whether these are errors or whether the reprises were due to different persons.

Item Thom*as* Mathowes for vi acres of errable land to Thomas Monyngton esquyer iis.
Item Johan Mydmore pay*e*th for halffe a yard land to the sayd chapter iiis. iiiid. ob.
Item the same Johane for the the same halff*e* yard land pay*e*th to John Warmecombe esquyer xd. ob.
[f. 44] Item ii acres to the cherche of Madeley iid.
Item John Hoppekyns payth for vi acres of errable land vid.

Tot*alis* exon*erantur per* Joc:[*obum*] Rogers & Ric*ardum* Veale [194]

S*umma* rep*r*ises xxis. iid. ob. p:
S*umma* clar*e* iiii £. vis. iiiid. ob.
cu*m* xxxviis. vd. gran*um* [195]
And xliii busshell*e*s of whete & xxx busshell*e*s off otes
S*umma* declar*e* cu*m* granyb*us* [*blank*]

Webtree: Madley: Obits

83. Obyttes ther Parochia de Madley
In p*r*imis iis. iiiid. goyng owte of c*er*ten landes belongyng to the p*ary*sshenor*s* ther meynteyn a obytte iis. iiiid. e:

Stretford: Birley: Morrow Mass Priest

84. The Land that Belongyth to the Morrowe Masse P*r*iest in the P*a*rysshe of Berley [196]
In p*r*imis Rychard Sherof holdyth iiii^{xx} acres of medo land*e*s leasowes & pasture xxvs. iiiid.
Item Will*iam* Sheroff of Bodnaham pay*e*the yerely owte of hys land*e*s in Longstrete Feld to kepe a lampe in the seyd churche iiiid.

S*umma* xxvs. viiid. p:
wherof

[f.44v] Rep*r*ises
In p*r*imis the seyd Rychard Sherof payeth yerely owt of the seyd iiii^{xx} acres to S*ir* Androwe Corbett viiis. e:

S*umma* declar*e* xviis. viiid. e:

Stretford: Staunton on Arrow: Our Lady Chantry

85. The Land*e*s that Belongyth to the Chaunt*ery* off O*ur* Lady in Staunton [197]
In p*r*imis Will*iam* Jenk*e*s for a ten*emen*te vis. e:
Item John Smyth for a tenemente iiiis. e:
Item Rychard Hall for a barn ~~& a plocke~~ in Staunton xiid. e:
Item off John Flecher for a ploke of ground ~~one ruge & ii buttes~~ vid. e:
Item John Badlond for on*e* medowe vs. e:

vend*untur* Thome Hungate & Aynsworthe [198]

Item Will*iam* Browne for ii p*a*rcelles of land viiid.

n*otatur* viiid. in m*a*nu domin*i* Reg*is*

S*umma* xviis. iid. p:

wherof: Rep*r*ises
In p*r*imis payd to ~~Master~~ ^ S*ir* Androwe [^] Corbett for a cheff rent out off a ten*emen*te of Will*iam* Jenk*e*s vid.
Item out of the same ten*emen*te to the lord*e*s of Staunton vid.
Item John Badland payethe out of a medowe to ^ the sayd S*ir* Androwe [^] ~~Master~~ Corbett id.

totu*m* exon*eratur per* d*ict*os Hungate & Aynsworth [199]

S*umma* rep*r*ises xiiid. p:

---

[194] This is a note (in the left hand margin of the previous page) bracketing all the reprises shown here above listed both on that page and this page.
[195] The grain total is included in the £4 6s 4½d. above. The grain total had been intended to follow 'cum granybus' but was then written in above.
[196] Although this is listed among other parishes of Webtree hundred, Birley was in Stretford hundred.
[197] Also in Stretford hundred.
[198] A bracket links all the preceding items.
[199] This marginal note is bracketed to include all three items.

Summa declare xvis. id. e:

Stretford: Staunton on Arrow: Lamps

[f. 45] **86**. Lampes ther

In p*ri*mis ther ys goyng owte of John Flechers land*es* yerely to kepe a lampe ther iiiid. e:

S*umma* [blank]

Webtree: Clehonger: Chantry

87. The Land*es* that Belongyth to the Chaunt*ery* of Cleh*a*unger [200]

In p*ri*mis Thomas Bayth*e* & Harrye Morgan for the farme of Much Crosse Cvis. viiid.

exon*eratur* [201] vend*itur* Joh*an*ni Hereford & Willyson

Item of Harrye Morvan cheffe rent vs. iiiid.

Item of the chaunt*ery* p*ri*est of All Seynt*es* in Hereford cheffe rent v*idelice*t the Rode Chauntre [202] vis. viiid.

~~*notatur* parcell of this Chauntre is sold to John Herefford & to Ric*hard* Willison [+++] videantur ?corp*ore* p*ar*ticulis~~ [203]

Item Thomas Parrocke for cheff rent vs. viiid.

Item Thomas Baughe for cheff rent xvid.

Item Will*iam* Mast*er* for cheffe rent ixd.

Item out of Harpers land cheffe xvid.

Item out of ? Chann*a*ce[204] land cheff rent viiid.

Item of the cherche of Morston cheff id.

Item of John Merrycke xxiis.

Item of John Howard xvis.

Item of Thomas Elsmarte xiis.

Item of ~~Harrye~~ Will*iam* Rygge xiiis.

vend*itur* Ja:[*cobo*] Rogers & Ric*ardo* Veale

Item of Rychard Pytte xs. e:

cu*m* p*er* alio*s*[205]

W*illelmo* Fountayne et Ric*ardo* Morice [+++]in l*itte*ris paten*tibus* ^ p*er* nomen [^] Agnet*is* Pytte ideo di*missus* [206]

Item the Chaunt*ery* House w*ith* the orchard & garden iiiis.

exon*eratur* ut vend*itur* Joh*an*ni Herefford

S*umma* [207] x £. ~~vis. vd. p:~~ vs. vid. p:

wherof:

[f. 45v] Rep*ri*ses

In p*ri*mis a cheffe rent goyng out of the land*es* in the tenure of Roger Pytte to the Quenes grace xxd.

Item to the erle of Shrewsbury oute of ~~Bede~~ Bedall*es* Halle xviis. id.

Item to the same erle owt of the ten*emen*te of Thomas Ellesmore ixs.

Item to the Kyng*es* maieste owt of the ten*emen*t of John Lysard p*ar*cell of the land*es* of Shene iis.

Et solu*tio* p*ro* barn [208] iiiis.

S*umma* rep*ri*ses xxxiiis. ixd. p:

---

200 None of the names of owners or occupiers of land below appear in the subsidy assessments for Clehonger, (vide *Herefordshire Taxes*). Some of the names appear nowhere in the county; others appear individually in other parishes. Thomas Baugh and Henry Morvan appear in the same parish—Lyde.

201 This is 'exon' which can only mean 'exoneratur', but, since this is an asset rather than a charge, it looks as if the discharges, usually recorded under 'Reprises'were here noted against the asset bearing the charge.

202 The last four words in a different hand added afterwards.

203 This note in the left hand margin may refer to the single entry above (the Rood chantry) or to the entire list (the Clehonger chantry). It extends by the side of this item and the next two items.

204 This may be the name 'Chaunce' miswritten.

205 This marginal note may refer to the item above although the line is opposite this item. It seems confused but may indicate that Rogers and Veale were not the only purchasers.

206 This note in the left hand margin is not wholly decipherable.

207 In the left hand margin an auditors' use grid or abacus shows the corrected total 'in dots'.

208 The meaning of this is hard to determine, but it may be a 'payment for a barn', which this editor has chosen. Its form however does not resemble an 'item' of charge like the rest.

Summa declar*e* viii £. xis. ixd. p:

Webtree: Holme Lacy: Obit

88. Home Lacye Obytte
In p*ri*mis on*e* acre of medowe lying [209] at Crymme gevyn by
one Wyllyam Graunger iis. e:
exoner*atur*. vend*itur* Joh*ann*i Cupp*er* & Ric*ardo* Traver

Webtree: Dinedor: Light

88a Dyndor
In p*ri*mis of John Sare one pounde of waxe out of c*er*ten land*es*
in hys tenure to fynd a lyght i lb of waxe iiiid. e:
vend*itur* Thome Hungate & Aynsworthe

Webtree: Preston-on-Wye: Chantry

89. The Land*es* that Belong to the Chaunt*ery* in P*re*ston
In p*ri*mis Thomas Dylyha gent holdyth ii mesuag*es* & a cotage
wi*th* c*er*ten land*es* Lxvs. xid.
vend*itur* Tho*me* Hungate & Aynsworthe
wherof

[f. 46] Rep*ri*ses
In p*ri*mis payd to the Dene & Chapyter of Heref*ord* a cheffe rent vis. ixd.
It*em* to the Dene & Chapyter of the comon backhouse vs. id. ob.
It*em* to S*ir* Mychaell Lyster knyght vs. xd.
It*em* to my Lord Ferrer*s* viiid.
It*em* to the Dene & Chapyter vid.
Totu*m* exoner*atur* p*er* eosdem
Summa rep*ri*ses xviiis. xd. ob. p:
Summa clar*e* xlviis. ~~id.~~ ob.

Webtree: Blakemere: Obit and Light

90. Blackem*er*
In p*ri*mis on*e* acre of pasture gevyn by Thom*as* Wynston oute of
Brownes Land to be prayd fore iiiid. e:
vend*itur* Thome Hungate & Aynsworth
It*em* iii acres of errable land in the tenure of Thomas Approsser to
mayntayn a lyghte xxd.
Summa iis. p: e:

Webtree Totals

[90a] S*um*m totall of the saide Chauntres Rep*ri*ses not deducted
xxiiii £. xviiis. viiid. e: p:
Reprises yerly ~~iiii £. xiis. vd.~~ ~~Cis. id.~~ iiii £. xis. vd. p: e:
And so remains ~~xix £. xviis. viid.~~ xx £. viis. iiid. [210]

Ex*aminat*a p*er* me Will*elmu*m Sayer deput*atem* Will*el*mi Crowch
Sup*er*vis*oris* *Dom*ini R*egis* ib*ide*m

[f. 46v] **[90b]** M*emorandum* that where yt dothe appere by the p*re*sentment of the
Ch*a*untre prest of Lynton called Our Lady Chu*r*che in the hundred of Greytre a
certeyn pece of land being in the hand*es* of Nicholas Jones the yerely value of
Cis. viiid. was p*re*sented by the said Chauntre prest there to be belongyng to the
said Chauntre the whyche p*re*sentment the said Nicholas hath proved by his honest
neyboures to be mad agaynst hym of very malice and evell will and not upon just
cause where he sayth that the said prest hath receyved no p*ro*fett*es* therof by the
space of this xx[ti] yeres.

---

[209] 'medowe lying' has been written over something else but only '.... land' can be read.

[210] This the total, less reprises, of all the Webtree valuations as well as the three Stretford valuations above.

John Scudamore's Totals

[f. 47] **[90c]** S*umma* tot*al*is Balli*v*at*i* Joh*ann*is Scudamo*r* Lxxiiii £. xvs. xd. ob. e: p:
Resolut*io*nes exeun*t* de possess*ionibu*s eiusdem ~~xii £. iiiid.~~ xi £. xs. viiid.
cu*m* xxs. in elemos*inis* e: p:
Et rem*anet* ~~Lxii £. xvs. vid. ob~~. Lxiii £. vs. iid. ob. [211] p: e:

[f.47v] [*blank*]

[f. 48] [212] **[90d]** M*emorandum* thys sum of vis. viiid. goyng out of a house in the tenure of John Thornecroft ys ~~out~~ charged in the totall sum*me* of O*ur* Lady Se*r*ves in Rosse for that the pr*ie*st ther nor eny other man to hys use have recevyd the seyd annuyte nor no pa*r*te therof by the space of thys xxv yerez &c.

[90e] M*emorandum* wher the pr*ie*st of the chaunte*ry* of Saynt George in Rosse hath p*re*sented that Will*iam* Dewe shuld pay out of a ce*r*ten leasowe xvid. by yere the same xvid. ys dyscharged out of the totall s*umme* of the seyd chaunte*ry* for that hyt have not be payd by the space of thys xx yeres &c.

[90f] M*emorandum* that wher yt was p*re*sented by the p*re*senters in the pa*r*ysh of Bellyngham that on*e* Will*iam* Skydmo*r* gent decessed gave a ce*r*ten pa*r*cell of land in the pa*r*ysh of Hentland in the tenure of one Elzabeth Jones to the valure of xiiiis. by yere the which pa*r*cell of land can not be valued abuve the s*umme* of xs. nor any man in the countrey wyll geve above the som*me* of xs. for hytt therfore yt ys ordered that she shall pay xs. yerely ffor yt to the kyng*es* use & the other iiiis. for to be remyttyd &c.

[ff. 48v, 49, 49v] *[blank]*

[f. 50] **[90g]** The Collectyon of John Incke [213]
The hundredes of Wolfey Wygmore Huntyngton & Stratford

[f.55v] M*emorandum* that the freechapell of Lytle Herefford lying w*ith*in the hundred of Wolfey in the countie of Heref*ord* being of the yerly value of viiis. viiid. by~~e~~ yere ys as the said John Ynke sayth yt ~~doth~~ is nott w*ith*in the statut for the said freechapell was dyssolved fyve yere before the said statut and the p*re*senter thereof dyd p*re*sent yt for malyce and therfore yt ys nott charged untill yt be better examyned.

canc*ellatur* [214]

[f. 56] The Collect*io*n of John Inke of the Hundred*es* of Wolfey, Wygmore, Huntyngton & Stratford. that is to saye, first

. Hundred of Wolfey

Wolphey: Leominster: Trinity Service

91. The Rentall of the Trynyte Servyce in Leomyster
In p*ri*mis ^ on*e* tene*men*te [^] in the tenure of Humffrey Strett gent by yere xvis. e:
vend*itur* Jo:[*hanni*] Pereant & Thome Reve
It*em* on*e* tenement in the tenure off ~~Thomas~~ David Thressher • vis.
vendit*ur* R*oberto* Carre
It*em* one closse in the tenure off Rychard Walton • vis. viiid.
vendit*ur* ut sup*ra*
n*otatu*r this close in t*enura* Ric*ard*i Walton ad vis. viiid. p*er* ann*um* is solde to R*obert* Carre by the name of a burgage or garden ut p*resentat* pa*r*tic*ule* osten*tate*
It*em* one ten*emen*te in the tenure of Rychard Pole vis. viiid.

---

[211] The total here of the three hundreds' individual net totals has apparently been adjusted for the error in the Greytree net total.

[212] All three items on this page have been crossed through, but in the interests of legibility in this edition have been left uncrossed through.

[213] The will of John Yncke of Leominster presented for probate on 25 Dec. 1549, (M.A.Faraday, ed. *Calendar of Probate & Administration Acts 1407-1550 in the Consistory Court of the Bishops of Hereford*, 549/47, 352).

[214] Note in the left hand margin, presumably referring to the struck through word 'doth'.

It*em* on*e* tenement in the tenure off Raffe Baker vs.
Item one tenement in the tenure off Thomas Butler viis.
Item one tenement in the tenure off Yevan Baker vis.
Item one garden in the tenure off Thomas Jonys iis. e:
vend*itur* Jo:[*hanni*] Periaunt & Reve
Item two ten*emen*tes in the tenure off John Wanklyn xiis. viiid.
Item one closse in the tenure off John Incke vis. e: p:
vend*itur* Perient
Item one tenement in the handes of George Colles [215] viis. xd. e:
vend*itur* Perient
Item a closse in the hand*es* off John Polle xxs.
Item a garden in the hand*es* off Edward Colbache xiiid. e:
vend*itur* Perient
Item one ten*emen*te in the hand*es* of Hughe Symond*es* vs.
Item one closse in the hand*es* off Phylypp Scarlet iiiis. e:
vend*itur* Jo:[*hanni*] Perent
Item a tenemente in thand*es* of Rowland Mylward viiis.
Item a tenement in the tenure of on*e* Owen xs.
Item one tenement in the hand*es* of John Coke vis. viiid.
vend*itur* ut sup*ra*
Item one tenement in the tenure off Hewgh Coffyn xiiis. iiiid.
Item one ten*emen*te in the tenure off Walter Caldwall xiiis. iiiid.
Item one tenement in the tenure off John Powell xiiis. iiiid.
Item one ten*emen*te in the tenure of John Lewe viis.
Item ii acres off errable grounde in the tenure of John Hylsley • xiid. e:
vend*itur* Jo:[*hanni*] Perient
Item ii acres off errable land in the hand*es* of John Stephyns • xiid. e:
Item one acre off errable lande in thand*es* of Thomas Wanklen vid. e:
Item one acre off errable grounde in the hand*es* of John Awalton vid.
vend*untur* Jo:[*hanni*] Perient [216]
Item one ten*emen*te in the tenure off John Moryce gent
w*hi*ch yeldeth every ii yerez xls. & the thryd yere danyd theretall [217] xxvis. viiid.
vend*itur* ut sup*ra*
[*Total*] x £. xiiis. iiid.
wherof

[f. 56v] Rep*rises*
In p*ri*mis payd out of the tenement aforsayd to the kyng*es* maiestye xxvs. viid. ob.
Item p*ai*d out off Toncrofte to the kyng xs. viiid.
vend*itur*
Item p*ai*d oute off the ten*emen*te that Walter Caldwey dwellyth in
the churche of Crystland [218] to fynd a lampe iis.
Item payd to Edmu*n*d Foxe gentylman iis. id.
Item to Roger Acton off Boculton vid.
Item to the heyrez off the Dalabers iiid. ob.
~~Item to the Saynt Mary service xxd.~~
q*uia* oner*atur* infra s*ummam* totall*is* p*re*d*ictam* [219]
[*Total reprises*] xlis. ~~xd.~~ iid. p:
S*umma* clara viii £. ~~xs. vd.~~ xiis. id. p:

Wolphey: Leominster: Our Lady Service

91a. O*ur* Ladye S*er*vys in Leomyster
Item a barn in the tenure of John Hynsley Liiis. iiiid.
vend*itur* Joh*ann*i Perient & Reve

[215] Written over a now unreadable name.
[216] The three preceding items were bracketed to this note.
[217] Unclear; could be 'denied ???' or 'Davyd ???'. There seems to have been no one in Leominster at the time bearing a surname like this. The figures however show that rent was paid only two years in three.
[218] 'Crystland' may be a misreading (from an antecedent document) of 'Erysland'. that is, Eardisland, a parish close to Leominster.
[219] The total, which the exigencies of clear lay-out require should follow in this edition, in the original is in the right hand margin and therefore above.

It*em* a howse in the tenure off the Vycaries Strett iiiis.
It*em* of John Hayes by yere for a closse & ii gardens xiiis.
It*em* of John Poll the yonger for a shoppe viiis.
It*em* off Thomas Maskall for hys howse xiiis. iiiid.
It*em* off Eln*or* Awellyn for hy~~s~~ r howse xiis.
It*em* off John Poll for vacant grounde in the Hyestrete xviiid.
It*em* of Davyd Morice for ii gardens iiis. vid. e:

vend*itur* Jo:[*hanni*] Perient

It*em* Nycolas Glov*er* for hys howse xs.
It*em* off John Poll thelder & Morice Vicaras for v acres of land iis. vid. e:

vend*itur* ut sup*ra*

It*em* off Belwyn of Stocton for on*e* acre off grasse iis.
It*em* a plock of grounde at Ivyngton in the tenure of John Addyes vid.
It*em* off Colbache for a garden xiid. e:
It*em* off Rychard Long for a medowe grownd xiid. e:

vend*untur* d*ic*to Joh*ann*i Perient

It*em* of Wyllyam Badny*n*che for a closse & a ruge xiid.
It*em* off George Monows iis.
It*em* off Wanck*e*lyns wyffe for a garden grounde iiiid.
It*em* off goodwyffe Sebryght vid.
It*em* of John Mores for a plot of grownd vs. [220]
[f. 57] It*em* off Walter Wateston for a garden xviiid.
~~It*em* off Nycholas Baylye xvid.~~

ca*n*cell*atur* q*uia* on*er*at*ur* in S*er*vic*i*a Be*at*e Marie voc*ata* O*ur* Lady Pyte in Leomyster [221]

It*em* off John Stephyns i lb. of waxe iiiid.
It*em* of Hewe Mathewe xvid.
~~It*em* owt off the Trynyte S*er*vice xxd.~~

q*uia* on*er*at*ur* in cantar*ia* S*an*cte Trinitat*is*

~~It*em* off John Addys Pet iis.~~
~~It*em* off O*ur* Ladye of Peters S*er*vice xiid~~.
It*em* of John Shotte vid.
It*em* of John Season vid.
It*em* off John Poole seni*or* vid.
It*em* off Davy Locar vid.
It*em* off Rychard Perryn iiiid.
It*em* off Roger Bourche xiid.
It*em* off John Pole the yonger xiid.
It*em* John Pates off Hen*or* xiis.
It*em* of John Payn iiiid.
It*em* off Harry Sheward vs.
It*em* off Hewe Halward xvid.
John Addys for a cotage iis.

[*Total*] ~~viii £. vis. vd~~. ~~viii £. iiiis. vd~~. viii £. iis. viiid. p: [222]

wherof: [223] Repryses
It*em* paid to the kyng*es* maieste xiis. viiid. ob.
It*em* to the howse of late~~lie~~ Rychard Flewellyng nowe in the tenure of Walton viiid.

[*Total reprises*] xiiis. iiid. ob. p:

S*um*m*a* clare vii £. ~~xiiis. id. ob~~. ~~xs. vid. ob~~. ixs. ~~ob~~. iiiid. ob. p:

---

[220] This item added in a different hand.
[221] See below: Our Lady of Pity service.
[222] These totals appear on the previous pagewhere the lists on that page and this are bracketed to the total in the right-hand margin. In the left hand margin on the previous page an auditors' use grid which has been struck through appears to show £7 16s. 5d.; this almost certainly refers to the total on that page—before correction.
[223] The word 'wherof' appears twice—in the margin with the totals and again at the foot of the column of figures.

Wolphey: Leominster: Our Lady of Pity Service

92. The S*er*vys of O*ur* Ladye a Pyttye in Leomyster
The Rentall off all the lande*s* & ten*emente*s belongyng to the S*er*vice of O*ur* Ladye of Pyttye in Leomyster called Phylype ap Morgans lande*s*
It*em* one howse in the tenure off Will*iam* Dongcastell at ye rent xxs.
It*em* on*e* barn with a garden in the tenure of Nycolas Baylye vis. viiid.
vend*itur* Joh*anni* Perient
It*em* one pasture in the tenure of ~~S~~ Phelyp Nycolas viiis.
It*em* Thomas Gillam dyd geve by wyll a c*er*ten howse & a barn unto the seyd service for thy fyndyng of an obytt for ev*er* xvis.
[*Total*] Ls. viiid. p:
wherof:
[f. 57v] Repryses
It*em* to Oure Ladye S*er*vyce ~~iiiid~~.
cancell*atur* q*uia* non allo*catur*
It*em* to the kynge*s* ma*ies*ties baylis there out of the lande*s* by yere ixs. vid. e:
S*um*m*a* clare ~~xxxixs. xd~~. xlis. iid. e:

Wolphey: Richards Castle

93. Wolfey ~~Paroch*ia* de Ricarde*s* Castell cum xviis.~~
The Rentall of all the Lande*s* & Ten*emente*s gevyn in Feoffament to certayn Inhabyt*a*untes w*ith*in the P*ar*ysshe of Rycards Castell
It*em* off Thomas Wheler for a shoppe in Ludlowe xvis.
no*tatur* ist*i* xvis. in te*nura* Th*ome* Wheler vend*itur* Rob*erti* Carre & Joh*an*ni Almond ut q*uia* l*itte*ras pat*entes* [+++] & exon*eratur* xvis. in rep*risis* ? exentes de [+++]
It*em* off Thomas Phylypis for one garden in Ludlowe aforseyd iis. iiiid.
Ludlow [224]
It*em* off Roger Mascall iiiid.
It*em* off ^ John [^] Hunllond for a tenement iiiis. iid. e:
It*em* off Raffe Lowke for a mese xxixs. iiiid. e:
It*em* off Rychard Cowarn for a mese xvis. e:
It*em* off Robart Smallman for a mese vs. vid. e:
It*em* off Wyllyam Powton for a mese xxvs. vid. e:
vend*untur* Jo:[*hanni*] Perient & Reve [225]
It*em* off Thomas Tumkyns for certayn landes xviis.
It*em* off John Baylye for a rent comyng out of Hewe Chapys lande*s* iis.
It*em* off Rychard Daowis for a rent out off one acre of medo or pastur belongyng to the Gild [226] off Ludlowe iis.
It*em* of Rychard Fowle for a closse iiiid.
[*Total*] vi £. vid. p:
S*um*m*a* vi £. vid. e:
Repryses
In p*ri*mis payd to therle of Warwyck [227] for Lugge*s* lande viiis. e:
exon*eratur* p*er* p*re*fat*um* Joh*annem* Perient
It*em* payd to the baylye of Ludlowe xvid.
It*em* to the seyd Erle of Warwycke for Luck*es* lande*s* ixs.
exon*eratur* ut sup*ra*
It*em* to the graunge off Wygmore vid.
It*em* to Saynt Johns Frarye vid.
It*em* to the seyd Erle off Warwycke for Powtens ground*e* xviiid e:
It*em* to the seyd Erle for Smallmons ground*e* xviiid. e:
It*em* to the seyd Erle for Hollande*s* ground xviiid. e:
exon*erantur* p*er* d*ictum* Jo:[*hannem*] Perient [228]
[f. 58] It*em* for Nycolas Gillie id.

---

[224] 'Ludlow' appears twice.
[225] This marginal note is linked by a bracket to the preceding five items.
[226] The Palmers' Gild.
[227] John Dudley, earl of Warwick.
[228] This marginal note is linked by bracket to the last three items.

Summa repryses xxiiis. xid p.
Summa clare iiii £. xvis. ~~vd.~~ viid. p:[229]

Wolphey: Yarpole: Our Lady Service & Lamplights

94. The Servyce of Our Ladye in Yarkepolle & Lamp Lyghtes there
Item one tenemente in the tenure of Rychard Broune wythe the appurtenaunces xxvis. viiid. e:
Item Thomas Dyrrye ^ free rent [^] oute off one acre of lamp lyghtes iid. e:

Wolphey: Croft: Lamp

94a The Rentall off all the Rentes Charges geven out of certen mens landes as hereafter ensueth to the fyndyng off a lamp within the parysshe off Crofte
The Parisshe of Croft
Item owte off the landes of Margery the dougttur & heyre off Thomas Boddye lying in Nether Lye iiiis.
Item out of the landes of Rychard Powtepon[230] in Yatton xxiid.
Item out of landes of John Hyggyns in Yatton foreseyd xviiid.
Item out off the landes of John Taylour in the same towne viid.
Item oute of the landes of John Bodye in the seyd towne viid.
Item oute of the landes of Alis Taylour wydowe in ye seyd town iiiid. ob.
Item owt of the landes of Edmund Mathewe in the seyd towne iid. qa.
Item out of the landes of John Capyas in the same towne iid. qa.
Item out of John Tumkyns landes in the same towne iid.
Item off the landes off Roger Gowghe in the seyd towne id. ob.
Summa ixs. vid. ob.[231] p:

[f. 58v] Lampes

Wolphey: Lucton: Lamp

94b. Luckton in Decanato de Leomyster Lamp
Item one ruge of medowe grownd which was gevyn to fond a lampe called the Lampe Ruge nowe in the tenure off Thomas Baylye xiid. e:

Hope-under-Dinmore

94c Hoppe under Dynmor
Item gevyn by Thomas Nycolas to have certen massis in the church there by hys last well xviis. iiiid. remaynyng in the handes off thexecutors xviis. iiiid. e:
respectuatur

Summa totalis off the partyclers somes aforeseyd[232] [*blank*]

Hundred de Wygmor

Wigmore: Leinthall Starkes: Chantry

95. The Landes belongyng to the Chauntery of Lentall Starkes
Item John Wedewoode for a tenemente with thappurtennces viiis. viiid.
Item Harrye Thomas for a tenemente vis. viiid.
Item Ales Poston wedowe for a tenement iiiis.
Item Robart Hyggyns for a tenemente vis.
Item Johane Brace wedowe for a tenement vis. viiid.
Item off Edward Wynster a leasowe called Tedwalles xs.
Item John Bryggwater turnour for a parcell ^ of lond [^] of medo called ye Mere vs.

---

[229] An auditors' use grid in the left hand margin, introduced by 'notatur', gives £4 16s. 7d. It was therefore the immediate precursor to this correction.
[230] 'Richard Put-upon' looks almost too good to be true as a nickname. If it is not, then it is a copyists's misreading of some other name written on an antecedent document.
[231] These figures also appear in the right hand margin linked to the list of items with a single bracket.
[232] No figures are set out here. The actual totals are: £30 1s. 9½d, less reprises £4 7s. 10½d. = £25 13s. 11d.

Item of Harrye Hepkes for a p*ar*cell of ground at M*ar*kes Roke xiid.
• It*em* Roger Longford for a medowe called Wyrall*es* vs. e:
• It*em* John T^a[^]ylo*ur* for a medowe called Walsheme Acre vis. viiid. e:
• It*em* off Roger Longeford for Cla*r*kes Leasowe xs. e:
venduntur Jo:[*hanni*] Perient & Reve [233]
It*em* off Wyllyam Dale for Clark*es* Lesowe iiiis. viiid.
vend*itur* Rob*er*t*o* Carre
It*em* of Rychard Fowler for a lesowe vis.
• It*em* off John Bryggwater for iii acres off land iiiid. e:
• It*em* the same John for halfe acre off medowe xiid. e:
• It*em* off John Wegdewod for a medowe iis. e:
vend*untur* eisd*em* Peryent & Reve
[f. 59] • It*em* off Thomas Vale for ii acres of land vid. e:
• It*em* off Edmond Hopkyns for acre off errable land iiiid. e:
vend*untur* Perient & Reve [234]
It*em* off Olyv*er* Bodye for a rent goyng out of a medo of hys viiid.
It*em* for a ten*emen*te wherin dwellythe ^ Rowlande Herteley [^]
the chaunt*ery* p*ri*est vis. viiid. e:
vend*itur* Joh*an*ni Perient & Reve
It*em* for xviii acres of errable land in the occupac*i*on of ye seyd p*rie*st viiid.
S*um*m*a* iiii £. xvis. vid. [235] p:
Rep*r*ises
It*em* payd to the kynges maieste for cheffe rent xiis. viiid. e:
S*um*m*a* clare iiii £. iiis. xd. e: p:

Wigmore: Wigmore: Our Lady Service

96. The Landes belongyng to Our Lady Service in Wygmore
It*em* M*aster* Thomas Croft for a closse at the P*ar*k*es* Syde • iis.
It*em* a nother closse • iiis.
It*em* a nother closse • xxd.
It*em* a nother closse • iiis. iiiid.
vend*untur* Joh*an*ni Perient mi*l*iti Thome Reve [236]
It*em* Rychard Southall a mese & closse & shopp ixs.
on*eratur*[237]
It*em* John Kyng*es* howse at the pament ~~& the chamber under the shoppe in the tenure off Rychard Sowthall~~ + xiid. e:
vend*itur* Feld & Woodward
It*em* Rychard Park*es* howse xs.
on*eratur*
It*em* Wyllyam Patyes howse iiiis.
on*eratur*
It*em* a house that Rychard Bedowe dwellyth ^ nowe [^] in the
holdyng off Thomas Croft*e* viiis. viiid.
on*eratur*
It*em* a chamber over the Broke nowe in the tenure off S*ir* John • + iiis. e:
vend*itur* Feld
It*em* Rychard Gryffyth howse & a barn iiis. viiid.
on*eratur*
It*em* John Buckenyll*es* howsse vid.
on*eratur*
It*em* James Smart*es* howse vid.
on*eratur*
It*em* Edmond Patyes howse xiid.
on*eratur*
It*em* John Kyng*es* howse + viiis.
vend*itur* eid*em* Feld

[233] This note is bracketed to the previous three items.
[234] This note is bracketed to the previous two items.
[235] The valuations above add up to £4 12s. 6d. This leads to the suspicion that the list has been copied and an item omitted in error.
[236] This note is bracketed with the four preceding items.
[237] 'Oneratur' ('It is charged') seems to be the most likely extension of 'on' with a flourish.

Item for the howse at the tree iiiid.
oneratur

Item the garden att Colys Bore iid.
oneratur

Item of M*aste*r Crofte ~~for the~~ ^ a [^] house at the churche style by yere iiis. [238]
oneratur

[f. 59v] Item the burgage at the Place viiid. ob.
oneratur

Item Edward Legge for the newe feld & the medowe xxs. e:

Item ~~John~~ Thomas Tyl*our* for one acre errable vid.
vend*untur* Thome Reve & Joh*ann*i Perient mi*li*ti [239]

Item off Raphe Harryottes for acre off errable land vd.
oneratur

Item for John Gyllard*es* howse • iiiis. ixd. ob. e:

Item Davyd Lewys for hys howse • xis. e:
vend*untur* Ric*ard*o Felde & Woodward [240]

Item M*aste*r Croft a barn and a orchard iiis.

Item M*aste*r Croft for a medowe at the More xviiid.
vend*untur* d*ic*tis Reve & Perient [241]

Item owte off the Cha*u*nt*ery* Closse ^ belongynge to the sayd chauntrye [^] xiid.
oneratur

Item owte off Edmond Mathowes closse in Ludlowstrett vid.
oneratur

Item off Rychard Bedowe farm*er* off Buckehyll iiiis.
oneratur

Item off M*aste*r Croft for the halde byeng att Dyppe Seller xid.
oneratur

Item Margery Crome howse xiid.
oneratur

S*umma* tot*ali*s Cxiis. id. p: [242]

Wigmore: Leintwardine: Chantry

97. The Land*es* that Belongyth to the Chaunt*ery* in the Churche of ~~Leynterdyn~~ Lentwarden

Item on*e* ten*emen*te in the tenure off John Smythe	+	xxviis.
Item Thomas Palfrey a ten*emen*te	+	xxiiis. vid.
Item Johane Vaure a cotage		iiiis.
Item John Crofteley a ^ cotage [^] ~~tenemente~~		vs. viiid.
Item Wyllyam Mason a cotage		vs. vid.
Item Thomas Buck a cotage		iiis. iiiid.
Item John Slyders a tenement	+	iiiis. vid.
Item Rychard Longford a ten*emen*te	+	xiis. iid. ob.
Item Robart Palffrey a tenement	+	xxviiis. ~~id~~. ixd.
Item Davyd Longeford a closse	+	xis. vid.
Item Rychard Hethe a ten*emen*te		vis. viiid.
Item Thomas Grene a tenement		xxd.
Item a cheff rent owte off John Smythes land		viiid.
Item for ii shopp*es* adioynyng to the churche yard		iiiis.
[f. 60] Item off Wyllyam Turn*our* a cheffe rentte	•	xiiiid.
Item Will*iam* Hyggyns paythe a cheff rent out of hys land*es*	•	iis. iiid. ob.
Item Jeffrey Taylor for cheff rente	•	iid.
S*umma* [243]		vii £. iis. viid. p:

[238] In a different handwriting from the rest of the list.
[239] The note refers to the two preceding items.
[240] The marginal note brackets the two preceding items.
[241] This marginal note refers to the preceding two items.
[242] In the left hand margin, preceded by 'notatur' is a crossed out auditor's use grid which appears to show a total of £5 9s. 2d., presumably a superseded total.
[243] An auditor's use grid in the margin gives a total of £7 2s. 6d, although the dots are smudged.

Rep*ri*ses
Item p*ai*d owte of Thom*as* Palfrayz howse to ye lord of Ricard*es* Castell + xiis. xd. ob.
Item to the heyrez off John Wygmore + viiis. vid. ob.

S*umma* rep*ri*ses [244] xxis. vd. p:
exoner*antur per* Kynge & Almonde
S*umma* clare vi £. xiiiid. e:

notatur[+++] ist*ud* p*a*rcell*um* annotat*um* ut infra attingen*t*' int*er* se ad Cviis. vd. ob. p*er* annu*m* prima facie ?conc*editur* p*r*out int*er* al*ios* Rob*er*to Carre & Joha*nn*i Almonde hered*ibus* & assign*atis* ip*s*ius Ric*ardi* [245] Carre in p*er*p*etuu*m p*er* l*itt*eras R*egis* pat*entes* dat*as* xv° Julii A*nno* iii° R*egis* Ed*wardi* VI tenend*um* in socag*io* ut de man*erio* de Estgrenewiche absq*ue* p*ri*ma habend*um* exit*us* a festo ~~Anno iii~~ [is] Annunciationis p*roxime* ante dat*um* pred*ictum* & exoner*atur* [+++] xxis. vd. in reso*lutionibus* exentis de premissis &c v*idelice*t xiis. xd. ob. & viiis. vid. ob. [246]

Wigmore: Leintwardine: Lamps

98. Lamps & Landes in Lentwarden
Item Augnes Harres wedowe payth out of her ten*emen*te to fynde a lampe ixd.
And also vid. yerely payd oute of c*er*ten land*es* late in the tenure of Bryan Longford nowe in the tenure of John Hurley esquier vid.

S*umma* xvd. p:

Wigmore: Aymestrey: Stipendiary Priest

98a [247] The Land*es* that Belo*n*gyth to the S*er*vyce of the Stypendary P*ri*est off Aylmestre
Item John Taylo*ur* holdyth a ten*emen*te co*n*teynyng xv acres of medowe & pasture ixs. p:
Item Walter Smyth holdyth a barn & a closse iis. viiid.
Item John Bodye holdyth ii acres & half of errable land vd.

no*tatur* ...... ist*ud* p*a*rcell*um* ?conc*editur* ?in ? ten*ura* a S*ir* Rob*er*to ~~Carr~~ Kinge & Joha*nn*i Kinge hered*ibus* & assign*atis suis* imp*er*p*etuu*m p*er* l*itt*eras R*egis* pat*entes* dat*as* xii° Ap*r*il*is* anno R*egis* Edw*ar*di VI iii[tio] tenend*um* in socag*io* ut de man*er*io de Estgrenwich absq*ue* p*ri*ma habend*um* exit*us* a festo Mic*hael*is ultimo Et exon*eratur* xvid. ob. in reso*lutionibus* exen*tis* de p*re*missis &c vi*delicet* xiid. id. ob. & iiid.

S*umma* xiis. id. p:

Rep*ri*ses
Item John Taylo*ur* payth out to John Lynghen esquyer xiid.
Item John Smyth pay*e*the to John Gold id. ob.
Item John Bodye paythe Alexander Newton iiid.

S*umma* rep*ri*ses xvid. ob. p:
S*umma* clara reman*et* xs. viiid. ob. p:

Wigmore: Aymestrey: Lamp

99 Lampe Landes in Aylmestre
It*em* out of the land*es* of Edmond Stevyns toward*es* ye fy*n*dyng of a la*m*pe vid.
Item out of the land*es* of John Tomkes to mantayn a lampe xiid.

S*umma* xviiid. p:

---

[244] Auditors' use grid shows this total.
[245] 'Ric'; perhaps a mistake as 'ipsius' suggests Robert.
[246] This scribbled marginal note on the previous page is hard to read but the sense is that properties marked '+' in the list above were sold to Robert Carre and John Almonde and the heirs and assigns of Carre for ever by royal letters patent dated 15 July 1549 to hold in socage as of the manor of East Greenwich without first having the income (issues) from the previous Lady Day and with payments due from these premises discharged, that is, 12s. 10½d. and 8s. 6½.
[247] In the document this section is also headed '98'. The suffix 'a' has been added in this edition to distinguish them.

Wolphey and Wigmore Totals

[99a] *Summa totalis Hundredi* de Wolfe [248] the reprises not deducted

xlviii £. viis. ixd. ob. p: e:

Reprises — vi £. iiis. iiiid. p: e:

And so remains — xlii £. iiiis. vd. [*ob.] p: e:

[f.60v] Hundred de Huntyngton

Huntington: Eardisley: Priest [249]

100 The Landes gevyn by Master James Baskerfeld knyght to fynd a priest in Yerssley

Item in the tenure of Thomas Gybbons a mesuage & certen landes in Wotton	xxiiis. iiiid.
Item certen errable land in the tenure of Waltur Bergoghe	viiis.
Item a certen lande in the tenure of John Harpar	viiid.
Item in the tenure off Thomas Este for acre of ^ arrable [^] land	vid.
Item in thandes off James Baker a mesuage & certen landes ~~xvis~~	xvs.
Item John Baker holdyth att the Wooddes Eves certen landes	viiis.
Item George Stephyns holdyth a house & a medo & acre of lande	xs.
Item Wyllyam Ball a medowe	iiis. iiiid.
Item Walter Crompe ii closses	iiiis.
Item Margrett Jackett wedowe holdyth one medowe	vis. viiid.
Item James Baskurfeld esquyer holdythe a medowe	xs.
Item Walter A Farmore holdythe mesuage	iis.
Item Thomas Jenyng for a newe platte	xxd.

Summa iiii £. xiiis. ~~xd.~~ iid. p:

Huntington: Eardisley: Lamp

101. The Lampe Lande in Yeresley

Item ii acres errable in the tenure if Walter Crompe	xd.
Item iii acres of errable lande lying in the seyd parysshe	xviiid.

Summa iis. iiiid. p:

Huntington: Eardisley: Our Lady Service [250]

101a The Landes that Belongyth to the Service of Our Ladye in Yersley

Item a farme at Wotton	xxiiis. iiiid.
Item a farme at Nether Welston	xvs.
Item a farme at the Woodselves	viiis.
Item a farm at Over Sponne	viiis.
Item a medow at Nether Sponne	iiis. iiiid.
Item John Stevyns for a howse & landes	xs.
Item Watkyn Crompe for landes	iiiis.
Item John Jakard for a medowe	vis. viiid.
Item Knowelles medowe	xs.
Item Watkyn A Fornall for certen landes	iis.
Item of John Harpar rent	viiid.
Item Thomas Este i acre	vid.
Item Thomas Jenyns a closse	xxd.

Summa iiii £. xiiis. iid.

cancellatur *quia* oneratur antea per se

[248] These are the combined totals for both Wolphey and Wigmore hundreds.

[249] See 101a below.

[250] This section has been crossed through. The crossing through has not been replicated in this edition for reasons of legibility. The section is another list of the properties shown above under section 100, but some of the personal names have been spelled differently and some place-names are different. It appears that two lists were made at different times as this section was compiled before section 100; John Jackard above had died by the time section 100 was compiled and his widow took his place.

Huntington: Clifford: Chapel

[f. 61] **102** The Land*es* that Belongyth to the Chapel ~~of Aise~~ of Clyfford
Item Thomas Bellynton for a ten*emen*te & xxiiii acres of land & pastur*e* xiis.
Item Robart Hoell on*e* acre off errable land iid.
Item John Morryce holdythe on*e* close co*n*teynyng iiii acres iis. iiiid.
S*umma* xiiiis. ~~iiiid~~. vid. p: [251]

Rep*ri*ses
Item the same Thomas Bellyngton payth yerely to the kyng*es* ma*ies*te viiid. ob.
Item the same Thomas paythe to James Whytney iis. id. ob.
S*umma* rep*ri*ses iis. xd. p:
S*umma* declara xis. ~~vid~~. viiid. e:

Huntington: Kington: Our Lady Service

103. The Land*es* that Belong to O*ur* Ladye S*er*vyce in the P*ar*ysh Cherche of Kynto*n*
Item a yerly rent going oute of the land*es* of ye frehold of John Baskerfeld gentylman iis.
Item a yerly rent goyng oute of a medowe of John Skandherd viis. iiiid.
Item a yerely rent going oute of a ten*emen*te of ^ the sayd [^] John Skandered [252] vs. iid.
Item a yerely rent out of a closse of the seyd John Skandered vs. iiiid.
Item a yerely rent going out off a vacant ground of the seyd John iiiid.
It*em* a yerly rent going out of a medo & a closse in the tenure of David Wyd xxd.
Item a yerely rent going owt of a mesuage of Watken Hyggyns iis.
Item a yerely rent going owt of the freland*es* of Thom*as* Wev*er* iiiis.
Item a yerely rent going owt of the frehold of Roger Morice viiis.
Item a yerely rent going out of the land*es* of Edward Berrynton vs.
Item a yerely rent going oute of the frehold of Ellyn Deyose wedowe iiis. viiid.
Item a yerely rent going oute of the landes of Lylwall wedowe vs. viiid.
Item owte of a closse in the holdyng of John Baker bocher viis. xd.
Item a yerely rent going out of a mese of John David showmaker ixs.
Item a yerely rent out of a shop of John Clement iiis. xd.
Item a yerly rent going oute of the land*es* of Johan Baker wedo iis. viiid.
Item a yerely rent owte of the land*es* of Watkyn Smyth iis. iid.
Item a yerly rent owt of the land*es* of Lewys Tylor iiiis. iiiid.
Item a yerly rent out of the frehold of Ellyn Hergest wedowe xxd.
[f. 61v] Item a yerely rent going owt of the land*es* of Ryse Taylo*ur* iiis. iiiid.
Item a yerely rentt owt of a mese of Thom*as* Vaughan gent vs. vid.
Item a yerely rent owt of the land*es* of Nycolas Walwyn gent xiid.
Item a yerely rent going owt of the frehold of Rychard Amedowe iis. viiid.
It*em* a yerely rent going owt of a mese of the frehold of John Cleme*nt* xiid.
S*umma* iiii £. xvs. iid. p: [253]

Huntington: Kington: Lamp

104 P*ar*ochia de Kynton Lampe Landes
Item owt of a medo ~~of the frehold~~ off James Vaughan vid.
Item id. a yere going owte of ye land*es* of James A Knolles id.
[*Total*] viid. e:

---

[251] This figure is calculated in an auditors' use grid in the left hand margin.
[252] 'Skanderel' seems to have been written over.
[253] An auditors' use grid , although crossed through, gives this total.

Stretford: Pembridge: Our Lady Service

105 The Land*es* & Ten*emen*t*es* Belongyng to the S*er*vyce of O*ur* Ladye in the Churche of Pembrug*e*

Item John Rosse wev*er* holdyth [blank] ten*emen*t & certayn land*es* w*ith* thapp*ur*ten*a*unc*es* in Pembrig*e* xxiis. iiid.
Item Kat*er*yng Hunt*e* on*e* ten*emen*te & thapp*ur*ten*a*unc*es* in Pembryg*e* iiiis.
Item Thomas Copn*er* holdythe on*e* tenement wyth thapp*ur*ten*a*unc*es* iiiis.
Item Thomas Raice holdyth a ten*emen*te in Pembruge iiis. iiiid.
Item Robart Lechord gent holdyth a ten*emen*te viis.
Item Watken Peytewyn holdyth certen pastures in Lyon Hales vis. xd.
Item Thomas Copley [254] taylo*ur* holdyth a ten*emen*te xs.
vend*itur* Rob*er*ti Carre &c
Item Will*ia*m Connoppe payeth owt off hys land*es* in Lyon*shall* iiiis.
Item Thomas Weale payeth owte of hys land*es* in Broxwod viiid.
Item Margrett A Connoppe holdyth on*e* acre off medowe iis. iid.
Item Thom*as* Badland holdyth on*e* ten*emen*te w*ith* c*er*ten land*es* medowes leasows & pastures att Berrowe xls.
S*umma* Ciiiis. iiid. p:
Wherof

[f. 62] Redd*itus* resolut*i*
Item John Rosse pay*et*h out of hys ten*emen*te yerely to the kyng*es* maieste iis. iiid.
It*em* Kat*er*yn Hunt payeth out of the seyd ten*emen*t to the kyng*es* maiestye vid.
It*em* Thomas Copn*er* payeth out of hys ten*emen*t to ye kyng*es* ma*ies*te xiid.
Item Thomas Rosse payth out of hys ten*emen*t to the kynges ma*ies*te xiid.
Robart Leychord payeth out of hys ten*emen*te to John Halle iis.
Item Watken Peytewyn payeth owte of hys pastures to the Lord Ferres xviiid.
Item Thomas Hopeley payeth owt of a ten*emen*t to the kyng*es* maiestye iis. xd.
exon*eratur per* Rob*er*t*um* Carre
Item Margery A Connoppe payeth owte off her ten*emen*t & acre of medowe to the k*in*gs ma*ies*tie iid.
Item Thomas Baland [255] payeth owte of the seyd ten*emen*t to the kynges maiestye xviiis. iiiid.
Item the same Thomas payeth owte of the seyd ten*emen*te to Rychard Ynkpen esquyer xxd.
S*umma* rep*ri*ses xxxis. iiid. p:
Et sic remenet claro Lxxiiis. e:

Stretford: Pembridge: Trinity Service

106 The Land*es* Belongyng to the S*er*ves of the Trynyte in the P*ar*ysh of Pembruge
Item John ap Hoell holdyth c*er*ten land*es* meadowes leasowes & pastures xxxiiiis. vid. e:
Item John Baker holdythe a ten*emen*te in Hynton ixs. viid. ob. e:
[*Total*] [256] xliiiis. id. ob.
vend*untur* Joh*an*ni Perient mil*i*[ti] & Thome Reve
S*umma* ~~xxxiis. id. ob.~~ ~~id. ob~~. xliiiis. id. ob. p:
wherof

[f. 62v] Reddit*us* resolut*i*
Item the seyd John Hoell owte of the seyd ten*emen*te to the kyng*es* maieste xis. vid.
Item the seyd John Baker payethe owte of the seyd ten*emen*t to the kyng*es* maieste for cheffe rent xixd. ob.
S*umma* rep*ri*ses ~~xiiis. id. ob~~. p:

254 This may be a mishearing for 'Hopley'; see reprises below.
255 'Badland' intended.
256 The total is both in the right hand margin and set at the foot of the list.

cancellatur quia extinguitur venditur ?unione possessio

Et sic remenet claro [257] xxxis. p:

Stretford: Weobley: St. Nicholas's Service

107 The Landes Belongyng to the Serves of Seynt Nycholas in Webbeley

Item the manor off Black Hall	Liiis. iiiid.
notatur redditus manerii de Blakehalle nisi xlvis. viiid. per annum e: ?relatione computi	
Item William Crowse	xxvis. viiid.
Item off Wyllyam Shater	xiis.
Item off Harrye Parteruge	vs.
Item off William Crowse	ixs. iiiid.
Item off John ^ Parteruge [^] ~~Jenkyns~~	iis. id.
Item John Hydd	iiiis.
Item off Symon ap Jenkyn	viiis. vid.
Item William Downe	iiis.
Item Jeffrey Hoelles for Fornall	iiiis. viiid.
Item the priest mencyon howse	viiis.
Item a Scolle Howse	xiid.
Summa	vi £. xviis. viid. p:
wherof: Redditus resoluti	
Item payd to the Lord Ferres for a cheffe rent	iiiis. vid.
Summa reprises	iiiis. vid. e:
Et sic remanet claro	vi £. xiiis. id. e:

Stretford: Weobley: Our Lady Service

[f. 63] **108** The Landes that Belongythe to Our Ladye Servyce in Webbeley

Item the howse that West dwellythe in the rent	iiiis.
Item a howse ~~by the broke~~	iiiis.
Item a closse in the Backe Lane	vid.
Item a howsse in the Hye Strett	xxd.
Item a howse that John Glover holdythe	iiiis.
Item a shopp Master Tomkyns holdythe	xvid.
Item a howse that Margrett Tanner holdythe	iis. vid.
Item a howse upon the Knappe	iis.
Item Our Ladye garden	xiid.
Item a garden place that John Lewes holdythe	vd.
Item a howse in the tenure of Jeffrey Kynnersley	iis.
Item a burgage in the Medowe Strett	iis. iiiid.
Item a garden by John Whetstone howse	vid.
Item Our Ladye medowe	xviis. vid.
Item x acres off errable land	vs.
Item a burgage in the tenure off Hewe ap Resse	iis. viiid.
Item i acre of pasture in Lyttle Sarnesffeld	iid.
Item Tanner howse	iis.
Item a burgage	vid.
Summa	Liiis. ~~iid~~. id. p:
Redditus resoluti	
Item to the Lord Ferres	xviis. vid.
Item to Master Monyngton	iiiid.
Item to the Lord Ferres	id. ob.
Summa reprises	xviis. xid. ob. p:
Et sic remenet claro	xxxvis. id. ob. p:

[257] An auditors' use grid appears to give a total of 21s. The total of 31s. precedes the cancelling of the reprises above.

Stretford: Weobley: Holy Rood

109.	The Land*e*s thatt Belongythe to the Roode in Webbeley	
	It*e*m a howse in the Medowe Strett	iiis. viiid.
	It*e*m a howse that Katryn Bromyard ^ hathe [^]	xiid.
	It*e*m a howse thatt Taylo*ur* hathe	iis. iid.
	It*e*m one burgage	xiid.
	S*umma* viiis. xd. p: wherof	
[f. 63v]	Reddit*us* resolut*i* [258]	
	It*e*m for cheffe rent	vs. iid.
	S*umma* repr*is*es	vs. iid. e:
	Et sic remanet claro	iis. viiid. e:

[64v] **109a** After my hartie commendac*i*ons whereas John Wall one of the king*e*s Maiesties buttery hath in lease of the kinges maiesties gyfte und*er* the seale of this court the chantryes of Kingesland and Dylwyn in the countie of Hereford, Letting you to understande that the same John Wall hath a graunte made unto hym for the p*ur*chasing thereof wherefore these are to requyre you furthwith upon the sight hereof to make ~~out~~ a note in yo*ur* bokes that the said John hath a graunte thereof and that you do not make or delyv*er* any p*ar*ticlers hereof to any p*er*son or p*er*sons but onely to the said John Wall the bringer hereof althoughe For any other shuld unadvysedly signe any warrante for the p*ar*ticlers of the same wherby the said John Wall might be prevented or hyndered in his sute Thus fare you well from my howse in London the xii[th] of June 1552.

Your lovinge frend Ric Sakevyle [259]

[ff. 64-65v] [blank]

Stretford: Kingsland: Services

[f. 63v] **110** The Land*e*s that Belongythe to the Servesses in the P*ar*yshe of Kingesland	
It*e*m in the tenure of Thom*as* Colman a ten*emen*t in Ov*er* Lawton	xxiiis. iiiid.
It*e*m off Will*ia*m ap Gw*il*l*y*m for a p*ar*cell of medowe ground	vs. iiiid.
It*e*m off Rychard Colman for a rent comyng owt of hys frehold	xiiid.
It*e*m off Thomas Colman for a ten*emen*te called Beddowes	xxixs. iiiid.
It*e*m off John Taylo*ur* for on*e* acre of medo in Brod Medowe	xiid.
It*e*m off Thomas Pyvynch for ii acres of medowe in Brod Medowe	iiis.
It*e*m off John A Knyll for a mesuage w*ith* thapp*ur*ten*a*unc*e*s called Rodes Ground	xxs.
It*e*m off Walter Mascall a p*ar*cell off medowe called Wylman Shyre	xiis.
It*e*m off Harry Roweall for a ten*emen*te & iii acres of land called Inchem*ar*sshe	viis.
It*e*m off Thomas Pyvynche ~~bucher~~ for a p*ar*cell of past*ure*	xviiid.
It*e*m off Thomas Henound of Marton for c*er*ten land	xxiis. viiid.
• It*e*m off Humffrey More nowe decessed [260] for a medowe plocke in Lyddicotte	vd.
+ It*e*m off Thomas Colman for a closse called S*ir* Thom*as* Closse	iiis.
+ It*e*m off Thomas Taylo*ur* & John Colman for on*e* past*ure* called Lane Sych*e*	xis.
It*e*m off John Kyngton for a p*ar*cell of medowe wh*i*ch rent ys for drawen for the space of viii yeres	iis. viiid.

[258] Relating to Weobley Holy Rood Chantry, section 109.

[259] This letter is an intrusion and difficult to place. In the interests of editorial clarity that part of f. 63v which relates to Weobley Holy Rood (section 109) has here been separated from the rest, which relates to Kingsland services. (section 110), and the letter and address placed between them. They could have been placed before f. 67 (section 113) since the marginal note referring to John Wall may be the subject of the letter. Sackvile was appointed chancellor of the court of Augmentations 24 Aug. 1548, (*CSPD, Edw. VI*, 432n.).

[260] Humfrey More of Shobdon made his will 16. Feb. 1547 and was dead before June that year, (*Hereford Probates*, 547/28, 344).

[f. 66] [261] Item off John a Knyll gent for a p*ar*cell of medo lying in Brod Medowe the rent theroff hath ben w*ith*drawen these vi yeres & more xxiid.

Item of Thomas Pyvynch for on*e* pasture called Hockblock the rent therof hath*e* ben w*ith*drayn iii yeres or ther aboute*s* iis. viiid.

Item off Thom*as* Pyvynch bocher for a p*ar*cell of medowe lying in Brod Medo ye rent theroff hath ben w*ith*drayn x yeres & a bove viiid.

Custum*ary* Ten*a*unnt [262]

Item Will*iam* Wall for a closse called Coties off the quenes custom hold w*ith* the custom rent*es* dew to the quene vis.

Item off Walter Loggar & Ales Frema*n* for c*er*ten acres off errable land & pastur*e* costom hold ixs.

+ Item a howse peynted for a scolle howse p*ar*cell off the quenes custom ground vis.

+ Item off Thomas Stevyn for a cotage of the custom hold called Hylles Howse viiis.

+ Item off Rychard Deswall for a ten*emen*t with thapp*ur*ten*a*unces & c*er*ten land*es* called Sedmolles xis. iiiid.

Item of John Kyngton for a pastu*r* called Howlward the rent hath w*ith*drayn v yeres & more vis. viiid.

Item of John Unkle for iii acres of errable land the rent therof hath ben w*ith*drayn ix yeres & more vid.

S*umma* ix £. ~~vis. viiid~~. xvis. [263]

Reddit*us* resolut*i*

Item payed to the quenes grace xiid.

Item to the heyrez of John Monyngton xd.

Item to the quenes grace xiid.

Item to the heyrez of M*aste*r Monyngton xd.

Item to Wyllyam Berryngton iis.

Item to Will*iam* Gryseman vid.

Item to the quenes grace iis.

Item to John Inke ixs.

Item to the quenes grace for custom rent iis.

Item to the quenes grace for custom rent iis.

[f. 66v] Item to the quenes grace for custom rent iis.

Item to her grace for custom rent iis.

Item to her grace for custom rent iiiis.

Item to John Blunt gent for cheff rent viid.

Item to the quenes grace for cheff rent iis.

S*umma* rep*r*ises xxxis. ixd. p:

Et sic reman*et* claro ~~viii £. xiiiis. xid~~. ~~iiiis. iiid~~. viii £. iiiis. iiid. p:

Stretford: Kingsland: Lamp

111. Lampes in the P*ar*ish of Kynglande

Item one acre off land in the tenure of John Trump*er* to mayntayn a lampe iid. e:

Stretford: Dilwyn: St. Nicholas's Service

112. The Land*es* Belongyng to the S*er*vyce off Seynt Nycholas off the P*ary*sshe of Dylwyn Magn*a*

Item Thomas Fryser certen land*es* xlviis. vid.

Item Rychard Boweyar for certen land*es* xxxiis. vd.

Item John Patye for certen land*es* xvs. iiiid.

S*umma* iiii £. xvs. iiid. p:

[261] There were blank pages between the two parts of this parish valuation, on the verso of one of which was written Sackvile's letter (section 109a). For the purposes of this edition these sections have been re-arranged into a more logical and comprehensible order.

[262] This appears to be in the singular and is set in the margin against the item relating to William Wall. The following items however all appear to be customary tenancies so the caption has here been taken to relate to them all.

[263] An auditors' use grid , which is struck through, gives a total of £9 17s.

Redd*itus* resolut*i*
Item Thomas Gryffyth payeth to the lord of Dylwyn that ys
S*ir* John Seyntlowe & to S*ir* John Talbott iiiis. iiiid.
Item the same Thomas Fryser payeth to M*aste*r ^ Brocketon [^]
~~Lyster knyght~~ viiid.
Item the seyd Thomas payth to S*ir* Mychaell Lyster knyght iis. iid.
Item to M*aste*r Monyngton esquyer iiiid.
Item John Patye payeth to Sir John Talbott ^ & John Sentlowe [^]
for certen landes xxiid.
Item the seyd John payth to the chaunt*ery* p*ri*est of Dylwyn iid.
Item Rychard Bowyar payeth yerely for certen land*es* to S*ir* John
Seyntlowe & S*ir* John Talbott knyght*s* vs. iid.
Item the seyd Rychard payth yerely to M*aste*r Brocketon viid.
S*umma* rep*ri*ses xvs. iiid. p:
Et sic remane*t* clar*o* iiii £. e:

Stretford: Little Dilwyn: Chantry

[f. 67] **113**. The P*er*teynyng to the Chaunt*ery* in the Church of Dylwyn P*ar*va
Item Thomas Moun*t*ford payeth for c*er*ten land*es* in Dylwyn xxxixs. xd.
Item Thom*as* Rychard a c*er*ten mese in Hevyn xxvis. viiid.
Item Walter Bedford pay*e*the out of c*er*ten land*es* in Lyttle Dylwyn xvis. viiid.
Item Thom*as* Brayn payth for c*er*ten landes in ? Hevin vis. viiid.
Item Thomas Rosse payeth for certen land*es* in Newton iiis.
Item John Phelyp*es* for a howse & a garden in Webbeley vis. vid.
Item of Wyllyam Shutter payeth for c*er*ten land*es* in Henwod xvis. viiid.
Item John ap Thomas for a pese off ground*e* in Dylwyn iiid. [264]
Item John Patye for the Hyll Ground in Dylwyn iid.
Item of John Nycholl for a c*er*ten mese in Dylwyn iid.
Item James Blether for a closse there viiid.
Item for a quytt rent in John Bayses lande iiis.
S*umma* vi £. iiid. p:

n*otatu*r to staye the p*articlers* of this Chauntrey for
John Wall one of the king*es* buttery who hathe
the p*re*ference of the p*ur*chase thereof by M*aste*r
Chauncelors warr*a*unte annexed to the Chauntrey
of Kingeslande in the countie of Here*ford* as by
the same there apperythe &c Ideo &c [265]

Reddit*us* resolut*i*
Item Moun*t*forde pay*e*th yerely a cheffe rent to John Seyntlowe
& S*ir* John Talbott knyght vis. vid.
Item Thomas Rychard*es* pay*e*th yerely a cheff rent therof to S*ir*
John Seyntlowe & to S*ir* John Talbott knyght*es* vis. viiid.
Item Wyll*ia*m Shoter payth therof for a cheff rent to the seyd
John Seyntlowe & to the aforseyd S*ir* John Talbott xiiis. iiiid.
Item Thomas Brayn pay*e*th for the cheff rent to Sir Mychaell
Lyster knyght iiis. viiid.
Item John Phelyp*es* payth to the Lord Ferres xviiid.
S*umma* rep*ri*ses xxxis. viiid. p:
Et remane*t* declar*o* iiii £. viiis. viid. e:

Stretford: Little Dilwyn: Obits

114. Obyttes off Dylwyn Parva
Item a medo gevyn by Ales Hurst called Mayde More to kepe a obytt iiiis. e:

Stretford: Kings Pyon: Our Lady Service

114a. The Land*es* Belongyng to O*ur* Lady Serves in Kingspewn
Item Thomas Seburn for a pese of medow ground in Sutton vis.

---

[264] 'd' has been written over an 's.; that it was this way round is supported by the arithmetic.
[265] And see section 109a.

Item Roger Apewen for on*e* acre of medo & lesowes & certen land*es* vs. vid.
Item of Hew Stephyns for c*er*ten land*es* in Kyng*es* Pewen xiid.
Item of Thomas Sampson for halfe acre of errable land iiid.
Item of Harry P*ar*terug for c*er*ten land*es* xd.
Item of Wyllyam Crosse for v acres of errable land in Beurley xvid.
Item of Will*iam* Mason for a cheff rent out of hys land*es* in Pewn xiid.
[f. 67v] [old 64v] Item owt of the land*es* of Will*iam* Down to mentayn a lyght viiid.
S*umma* xvis. viiid. p:
Reddit*us* resolut*i*
Item payd owt of the same s*umma* viiid. e:
S*umma* rep*ri*ses viiid. e:
Et sic reman*et* declar*o* xvs. xid. e:

Stretford: Lyonshall: Our Lady Service

115 The Land*es* that Belong to O*ur* Ladye S*er*vyce in Lyonhalles
In p*ri*mis Will*iam* a More & Watter Bredd doth hold a past*ur* called Stockes Feld xxis.
Item David Ford holdyth v acres of land medo & pasture xiiis. iid.
Item Watter Traunto*r* holdyth on*e* medo cald Daysmore Medow iiis. xd.
Item Thomas Glov*er* holdyth on*e* burgage ~~att the Well~~ iis.
Item Rychard Symond*es* holdythe on*e* acre of land vis. viiid.
vend*untur* Jo*hanni* Perient mi*li*ti & Tho:[*me*] Reve
S*umma* xlvis. viiid. p:
Reddit*us* resolut*i*
Item Davyd Forge pay*e*th to the kyng*es* ma*ies*te for chefe rent xs. iiiid.
extinguit*ur*
Item the same Davyd pa*ie*the to the Lord Ferres for chef rent iid.
exon*eratur per* Jo*hann*em Perient & Reve
Item Watter Traunto*r* payeth yerely to the kyng*es* maieste vid.
extinguit*ur*
Item Rychard Symons path to the kyng*es* ma*ies*te for chef rent viid.
extinguit*ur*
Item the same Rychard pay*e*th to the Lord Ferres iis. iiid.
Item Thomas Glov*er* payeth to the Lord Ferres xiid.
exon*erantur* ut sup*ra*
Item Will*iam* More & Will*iam* Brydd payth yerely for a obytt xiid.
S*umma* rep*ri*ses xvs. xd. p:
Et sic reman*et* declar*e* xxxs. xd. e:

Stretford: Kinnersley: Schoolmaster

116. The Land*es* that Belongyth to the Scole m*aste*r or Stype*n*dary P*ri*est of Kynnersley
Item Thom*as* Sucker for the farm of Almelye w*ith* thapp*ur*ten*a*unces iiii £. viid. e:
vend*itur* Rob*er*to Thomas
Item Rychard Mathew for a ten*emen*t w*ith* thapp*ur*tenaunc*es* in Ayle xxxiiiis. iiiid.
vend*itur*
Item John Whytney for a ten*emen*te w*ith* thapp*ur*ten*a*unc*es* in Lytton Liiis. iiid.
vend*itur*
S*umma* ~~vii £. xviiis. iid~~. viii £. viiis. iid. [266]
Reddit*us* resolut*i*
Item payd owte of the sayd farm to the lord of Almelye xiiis. xid.
It*em* to S*ir* Mychaell Lyster knyght for a cheff rent out of the land*es* in Aley & Letton xviiis. iid.
Item to M*istress* Anne Corbett for a cheff rent going out of a past*ur* in Hurtesley xiid.
exon*erantur per* p*er*quis*atores*
Item to the kyng*es* ma*ies*te out of the seyd ten*emen*t in Letton iiis. id.
S*umma* rep*ri*ses declar*e* xxxvis. iid. p:

[266] The total is also shown in an auditors' use grid in the margin.

Et sic reman*et* declar*e* vi £. ~~ixs.~~ xiis. e:

Stretford: Kinnersley: Obits

[f. 68][old 65r] **117** Obyttes ther Kynn*er*sley
Item one yerely rent off vd. gevyn owte ^ of the landes [^] of the heyrez off John Carpent*er* for to kepe a obytte vd. e:
vend*itur*

Stretford: Eardisland: Lamp

118. Ereslande
Item ii galons off oyle owt of the land*e*s off the Trynyte in the parysshe off Leomy*n*ster iis.
Item one acre off land lying in Este Feld at Eresland to meynteyn a lampe in the tenure of Raffe Dyggas iiiid.
[*Tota*l] iis. iiiid. p:

Stretford: Monkland: Light

119 Monkland
Item c*er*ten land*e*s in the tenure of Watter Seward to maynteyn a lyght vs. iid. e:

Stretford: Shobdon: Lamp

120 Shobdon a Lampe
Item a acre off errable land in the tenure of Rychard Taylo*ur* to kepe a lampe iid. e:

Stretford: Almeley: Lamp

121 The P*ar*ishe of Almaley
Item one acr*e* of land in the tenur of James Robayge for a lamplight vid. e:

Huntington and Stretford Totals

[**122**] S*um* of the Chauntries in the Hundred of ~~Huntington~~ the rep*ri*ses not deducted
Lx £. ixs. iiid. ob. e: p:
Rep*ri*ses x £. vis. iid. p: e:
Rem*anet* L £. iiis. id. ob. e: p:

Ex*aminatur* p*er* Will*elmu*m Sayer deput*atem* Will*el*mi Crowch, Supervis*oris* Dom*in*i Reg*is* ib*id*em

[f. 68v] To my lovinge frendes the king*es* Ma*ies*ties Auditor and Surveyor of his grac*es* countie of Heref*ord* and to either of theym [267]

[f. 68v] Istud rental*e* dilib*eratu*m fuit ad manu*m* Jo:[*hannis*] Hanbie aud*itoris* p*er* manu*m* deput*atis* supervis*oris* xix Februarii a*nn*o iii^{cio} Reg*is* Edw*ardi* vi [268]

John Inke's Totals

[f. 69] [**123**] S*um*m*a* tot*ali*s Balli*va*t*i* Joh*an*nis Inke [269] Cviii £. xviis. id. e: p:
Resolut*io*nes ex*ientes* de possess*ionibu*s eiusdem xvi £. ixs. vid. e: p:
Et remanet iiii^{xx} xii £. viis. viid. e: p:

[267] This address would seem to preceded Sackvile's letter at section 109a, but, if it did, he was oddly placed.
[268] 19 Feb. 1549. The delivery note ought logically to come last, but it is likely that it was written on the penultimate page because it was blank.
[269] Incke's bailiwick included Wolphey, Wigmore, Huntington and Stretford hundreds.

HEREFORDSHIRE CHANTRY VALUATIONS OF 1547
INDEX

The index-numbers below refer, not to the pages of this volume, but to the (editorially adjusted) section-numbers within the text. * indicates more than one entry of the name in the section.

www.ingramcontent.com/pod-product-compliance
Ingram Content Group UK Ltd.
Pitfield, Milton Keynes, MK11 3LW, UK
UKHW051137260726
13967UKWH00010B/3111